Cennie L. Parmyster

For with God nothing
shall be impossible.
Luke 1: 37 KJV

The Signs of God
"ARE EVERYWHERE"

CONNIE L. PARMENTER

WESTBOW
PRESS
A DIVISION OF THOMAS NELSON
& ZONDERVAN

WestBow Press books may be ordered through booksellers or by contacting:

WestBow Press
A Division of Thomas Nelson & Zondervan
1663 Liberty Drive
Bloomington, IN 47403
www.westbowpress.com
1 (866) 928-1240

ISBN: 978-1-4908-2302-7 (sc)
ISBN: 978-1-4908-2303-4 (e)

Library of Congress Control Number: 2014900737

Printed in the United States of America.

WestBow Press rev. date: 01/10/2014

Contents

Dedication. . . . . *.xi*

Acknowledgments. . . . . *xii*

How I See God In Everything . . . . *.xiv*

Our Captain . . . . *xvii*

Introduction. . . . . *.xix*

More about the book. . . . . *xx*

Yellow Butterflies . . . . *.xxi*

Man's Problem 1

Satan, Sin, Hell. 2

Thought For The Day 3

Satan, Sin, Hell

Judgment 10

Thought For The Day 11

Judgment

Worry. 19

Thought For The Day 20

Worry

God's Love 24

We Cannot Work our way to God. 26

Fluffy Clouds 27
Help, Helper 29
Thought For The Day 30

Help / Helper

What A Beautiful Night 38
Love 40
Thought For The Day 41

Love

Christmas 50
Jesus, Christ 52
Thought For The Day 53

Jesus / Christ

God. 60
God has a Solution 62
Forgiveness, Grace. 63
Thought For The Day 64

Forgiveness / Grace

All Around The Town 69
Truth 71
Thought For The Day 72

Truth

Let Us Pause 81
Obey, Obedience. 83
Thought For The Day 84

Obey / Obedience

Trust. 95
Accept His Gift. 97
Faith, Faithful. 98
Thought For The Day 99

Faith / Faithful

October Harvest 111
Trust 113
Thought For The Day 114

Trust

God's Musical Creatures 121
Eternal, Eternity 123
Thought For The Day 124

Eternity/ Eternal Life

It's Then 130
The Result 132
Salvation 133
Thought For The Day 134

Salvation

God's Creation 141
Rejoice 143
Thought For The Day 144

Rejoice

Thanksgiving 148
Prayer 150
Thought For The Day 151

Prayer

Show Me The Way 159
Now what 161
Word Of God 164
Thought For The Day 165

Word Of God

The Preacher And The Lady 174
Witnessing 176

Thought For The Day 177

Witnessing

Choices 183
Thought For The Day 184

Choices

Choices And Changes 195

Plan of Salvation

Man's Problem 198
We Cannot Work our Way to God 199
God has a solution. 200
Accept His Gift. 201
The Result. 202
Now What?. 203
When you're out and about 206

Dedication

I'd like to dedicate this book to a dear friend Bob Atchison. A few years ago I told him I wanted to write, but I wasn't sure if it was just me or if it is something God wants me to do. He said, "Go for it, if it's not something God wants for you He'll let you know." Thanks Bob! Love and miss you.

I would also like to dedicate this book to my husband Ronald, our three children and to our five grandchildren Nathan, Rebekah, Carson, Michael, and Cali. I praise God for each one. I love you all.

Acknowledgments

First I'd like to thank God for this opportunity to tell others about Him and Jesus, and how they too can have Jesus in their hearts. And a special thank you to my husband Ronald for his help, patience, prayers and encouragements. And thanks to my brother Lloyd and his wife Sue, as they diligently worked to put passages of Scripture to many of the sayings. A special thank you to each of our children, Marcella and her husband Mike for all their prayers, suggestions, and encouragements. Sherry and her husband Lance for their prayers, encouragements, suggestions, and for very diligently going over all the sayings, Scripture verses, and categories to make sure they all fit together. Roger for his help, prayers, and encouragements, and suggestions. His wife Jennifer for her prayers, encouragements, suggestions, and especially for her proofreading parts of this book. Also I'd like to thank Candy a friend and my prayer partner for all her prayers and for helping proofread part of this book. For Joan for looking up some Scripture verses to go with some of the sayings. And for Pam for all her computer help. I'd like to thank all of my family and friends for all their help, suggestions, encouragements, and especially for all their prayers. I praise God for whoever's heart He burdened to send me two of the Bibles I needed for this book. And to those who gave financially, thank you and God Bless. A very special thank you to a ten year old girl named Alyssa Serri. She knew I didn't have any idea for a title to this book, after thinking and praying about it for a couple of weeks the Lord blessed her with the title. The Signs of God "Are Everywhere" I praise God for everyone who helped with, and especially for all the prayers that were said concerning this book. Without them and the Lord it would not have been possible. Praise God!

How I See God In Everything

THE SIGNS OF GOD "ARE EVERYWHERE" as you know is the title of this book. I'd like to share with you how I see God in everything and if you open your eyes and heart you can too. I'd also like to share with you how I know God and how you can also know God.

To begin with, when I get up the sun may be shining or not as it may be cloudy, raining or snowing. If the sun is shining you know it's from God, as man did not make the sun, nor cause it to shine. Then I hear the birds singing and as I look out my window I can see many different birds of various colors. Man never made the birds either or caused them to sing.

There are many different kinds of animals there are tame animals such as dogs and cats, cows and horses and wild animals such as lions, deer, elephants, bears, and many other wild animals. There are also different insects like flies, mosquitoes and many reptiles. God also created beautifully colored butterflies.

I also see God in the grass, flowers and the trees, and in the winter the green grass turns brown, the flowers die or go dormant and the trees lose their leaves. But when spring comes they all seem to come back to life.

Some days we have rain, sometimes just a little, and sometimes a lot and sometimes on one side of the road and not on the other. There are times when I hear thunder and see lightening. Then sometimes there are really bad storms like hurricanes and tornadoes. Many times after a rain I see a rainbow that God has put in the sky, with all of its beautiful colors. Man can't do that.

There are days when I see the snow coming down and in amounts from just a trace to inches to feet. Also some days when the temperatures are just right I see frost all over the ground and on cars and on rooftops. These things man cannot do either, Oh! Yes, man can make artificial snow for awhile with machines and also make frost. But they cannot do it in super large amounts and in different places as only God can do and all at the same time.

Then there is the moon, sometimes it's a full moon, sometimes it's a half moon and sometimes it's a sliver of a moon, and sometimes we don't see the moon for awhile. How does God do that? Then God has given us the four seasons, winter, spring, summer and fall. He gave us the wind and we can't tell where it comes from or where it is going. I have seen where the wind blew over a strip of corn in field and didn't even touch the corn next to it. Man can't do this.

He gave us the stars in the night sky. How did God hang them there and how do they stay put? God only knows. Yes! Sometimes I see a falling star. Why do some twinkle? I don't know. At the same time I can see planets in our solar system. God has also given us the towering majestic mountains. Man cannot do any of this either it is only something God can do.

What is God's reason for all of these things that man thinks may be good or bad? Maybe He wants to show us His miraculous power and possibly bring us to Himself.

God created you and me with love and with that same love He gave you and me Jesus Christ, His one and only Son to die on a cross for our sins, as we are all sinners, so that we might one day live in heaven with Him. I know God because I confessed to Him that I am a sinner and believed in my heart that He was raised from the dead and that He is in heaven preparing a place for me and one day He will come for me to live with Him forever. Praise God!

My prayer for you, as you read the rest of this book, is you will also see God in everything and that you too will invite Jesus into your heart and life but you must believe His word. How? Read the Bible each day with an open heart and pray for Him to show you.

Our Captain

Our Captain is our Master, our God, He is strong and He can defend and protect us from Satan's attacks. God knows when things go wrong He can help us and comfort our hearts if we let Him.

But we need to have Him in our hearts and lives so give your heart to God our Captain.

Our Captain

A Mighty Fortress is our God,
a defense that will never fail.
A rampart that we may hide behind,
and strength that will not quail.

Sometimes when life's battles are raging,
and seems as if all is gone wrong.
There comes this mighty Conqueror,
and fills my heart with a song.

I thank God for our wonderful Captain,
who gives us courage each day.
That whatever may confront us,
He will be with us all the way.

From my Stepfather
Homer Haley
Written—1980

Introduction

Over the past nine years, as my husband and I traveled across the country, we enjoyed the various sayings on church signs. About a year ago the Lord placed on my heart to put the more than 200 of these sayings into one book. With the Scriptures as my guide and with the help of others, the many organized sayings as well as an outlined plan of salvation all came together. It is my prayer that you will search these Scriptures and apply them to all areas of life. I also pray that many people would come to know the Lord through these writings! Praise God!

More about the book

This book is a little different than most, as you not only have how I see God in everything, you also have the sayings from church signs with Scripture verses, also before each poem I have included a comment on that poem. And I have included the plan of salvation throughout. I have included before each category a comment on that category and a thought for the day page.

Yellow Butterflies

Did you ever think about where the butterflies come from in the spring, summer and early fall? It seems like they just appear out of nowhere, then when it gets cold they just seem to disappear again until spring. Isn't it something how they know when to come and when to go? God is amazing!

Yellow Butterflies

In the summer, fall and spring,
yellow butterflies the Lord does bring,
as I look out my window flying so free,
or go for a walk yellow butterflies I see.
They chase each other to and fro,
in the winter, Lord! Where do they go?

Connie L. Parmenter

Man's Problem

No matter what you have done in your life, or how much good you have done, or how much you have served or given money to help others, we all have the same problem—we are separated from God.

2It's your sins that have cut you off from God. Because of your sins, he has turned away and will not listen anymore.

Isaiah 59:2 (NLT)

It does not matter to God if you only told a little white lie, or committed murder. It is all sin—and we have all sinned.

23For everyone has sinned; we all fall short of God's glorious standard.

Romans 3:23 (NLT)

He cannot allow sin in His presence. Worse yet, there is a penalty for sin.

23For the wages of sin is death, but the gift of God is eternal life in Christ Jesus our Lord.

Romans 6:23 (NIV)

Satan, Sin, Hell

Satan is a crafty fellow, and if you don't keep your mind and heart on the Lord, he will deceive you and try to draw you to himself.

When we do wrong things, and think wrong thoughts this is sin. But Jesus can forgive us all of our sins. But we must first confess our sins to Him and ask Him into our hearts.

Thought For The Day

Think about where you will spend eternity.

Will it be in heaven with Jesus or in hell with Satan?

Satan, Sin, Hell

If you die lost, you are a loser.

41 "Then He will also say to those on the left hand, 'Depart from Me, you cursed, into the everlasting fire prepared for the devil and his angles:

46And these will go away into everlasting punishment, but the righteous into eternal life."

Matthew 25:41, 46 (NKJV)

22 Many will say to Me in that day, 'Lord, Lord, have we not prophesied in Your name, cast out demons in Your name, and done many wonders in Your name?' 23 And then I will declare to them, 'I never knew you; depart from Me, you who practice lawlessness!'

Matthew 7:22—23 (NKJV)

36 For what will it profit a man if he gains the whole world, and loses his own soul? 37 Or what will a man give in exchange for his soul?

Mark 8:36-37 (NKJV)

25 For what profit is it to a man if he gains the whole world, and is himself destroyed or lost? 26 For whoever is ashamed of Me and My words, of him the Son of Man will be ashamed when He comes into His own glory, and in His Father's and of the holy angles.

Luke 9:25-26 (NKJV)

Give Satan an inch and he'll be your ruler.

6 And the devil said to Him, "All this authority I will give You, and their glory; for this has been delivered to me, and I give

it to whomever I wish. 7 Therefore, if You will worship before me, all will be Yours." 8 And Jesus answered and said to him, "Get behind Me, Satan! For it is written, 'You shall worship the Lord your God, and Him only you shall serve.' " Luke 4: 6-8 (NKJV)

44 You are of your father the devil, and the desires of your father you want to do. He was a murderer from the beginning, and does not stand in the truth, because there is no truth in him. When he speaks a lie, he speaks from his own resources, for he is a liar and the father of it.

John 8:44 (NKJV)

8 Be sober, be vigilant; because your adversary the devil walks about like a roaring lion, seeking whom he may devour.

1ˢᵗ Peter5:8 (NKJV)

Sin has no minimum wage the wages of sin is death.

16 Don't you realize that you become the slave of whatever you choose to obey? You can be a slave to sin, which leads to death, or you can choose to obey God, which leads to righteous living.

Romans 6:16 (NLT)

23 For the wages of sin is death, but the gift of God is eternal life in Christ Jesus our Lord.

Romans 6:23 (NIV)

For every sin, Satan has an excuse.

44 You are from your father the devil, and you choose to do your father's desires. He was a murderer from the beginning and does not stand in the truth, because there is no truth in him. When

he lies, he speaks according to his own nature, for he is a liar and the father of lies.

John 8:44 (NRSV)

Good without God equals—0-.

10 as it is written: "There is no one who is righteous, not even one; 12 All have turned aside, together they have become worthless; there is no one who shows kindness, there is not even one."23 since all have sinned and fall short of the glory of God;

Romans 3: 10, 12, 23 (NRSV)

Hell has no fire escape.

41 "Then the King will turn to those on the left and say, 'Away with you, you cursed ones, into the eternal fire prepared for the devil and his demons.

Matthew 25:41 (NLT)

29 but anyone who blasphemes the Holy Spirit will never be forgiven. This is a sin with eternal consequences."

Mark 3:29 (NLT)

Forbidden fruit causes sticky jams.

12 Therefore, just as though one man sin entered into the world, and death through sin, and so death spread to all men, because all sinned—

19 For as through the one man's disobedience the many were made sinners, even so through the obedience of the One the many will be made righteous.

Romans 5: 12, 19 (NASB)

There would be no gossiping tongues, if there were no gossiping ears.

13 A talebearer reveals secrets, But he who is of a faithful spirit conceals a matter.

Proverbs 11:13 (NKJV)

13 And besides they learn to be idle, wandering about from house to house, and not only idle but also gossips and busybodies, saying things which they ought not.

1st Timothy 5:13 (NKJV)

Judgment

Judgment day is a day we will all go through standing before God. We will be judged on what we have done for the Lord, or what we have not done. And we will be judged whether we have asked Jesus in our heart or not.

Thought For The Day

So consider how you will be judged as God already knows your heart. Ask Him and He can change your heart today for good.

Judgment

The world is so rich in delusion, that the truth is priceless.

25 They exchanged the truth of God for a lie, and worshiped and served created things rather than the Creator—who is forever praised. Amen.

Romans 1:25 (NIV)

8 If we say that we have no sin, we deceive ourselves, and the truth is not in us.

1st John 1:8 (NRSV)

Hell has no exit, Heaven needs none.

19 " There was a certain rich man who was clothed in purple and fine linen and fared sumptuously every day. 20 But there was a certain beggar named Lazarus, full of sores, who was laid at his gate, 21 desiring to be fed with the crumbs which fell from the rich man's table. Moreover the dogs came and licked his sores. 22 So it was that the beggar died, and was carried by the angels to Abraham's bosom. The rich man also died and was buried.

23 And being in torment in Hades, he lifted up his eyes and saw Abraham, afar off, and Lazarus in his bosom. 24 "Then he cried and said, 'Father Abraham, have mercy on me, and send Lazarus that he may dip the tip of his finger in water and cool my tongue; for I am tormented in this flame.'25 But Abraham said, 'Son, remember that in your lifetime you received your good things, and likewise Lazarus evil things; but now he is comforted and you are tormented. 26 And besides all this, between us and you there is a great gulf fixed, so that those who want to pass from here to you cannot, nor can those from there pass to us.'

Luke 16:19-26 (NKJV)

If you can't stand the heat believe in Jesus.

10 Then the devil, who had deceived them, was thrown into the fiery lake of burning sulfur, joining the beast and the false prophet. There they will be tormented day and night forever and ever. 11 And I saw a great white throne and the one setting on it. The earth and sky fled from his presence, but they found no place to hide. 12 I saw the dead, both great and small, standing before God's throne. And the books were opened, including the Book of Life. And the dead were judged according to what they had done, as recorded in the books. 13 The sea gave up its dead, and death and the grave gave up their dead. And all were judged according to their deeds. 14 Then death and the grave were thrown into the lake of fire. This lake of fire is the second death. 15 And anyone whose name was not found recorded in the Book of Life was thrown into the lake of fire.

Revelation 20: 10—15 (NLT)

Religion is just a mask you wear, and God knows where you are.

10 "I the Lord search the heart and examine the mind, to reward a man according to his conduct, according to what his deeds deserve."

Jeremiah 17:10 (NIV)

21 Would not God find this out? For He knows the secrets of the heart.

Psalm 44:21 (NKJV)

Burying one's talents is a grave mistake.

24 "And the one also who had received the one talent came up and

said, 'Master, I knew you to be a hard man, reaping where you did not sow and gathering where you scattered no seed.

25 'And I was afraid, and went away and hid your talent in the ground. See, you have what is yours.' 26 " But his master answered and said to him, 'You wicked, lazy slave, you knew that I reap where I did not sow and gather where I scattered no seed. 27 'Then you ought to have put my money in the bank, and on my arrival I would have received my money back with interest. 28 'Therefore take away the talent from him, and give it to the one who has ten talents.' 29 " For to everyone who has, more shall be given, and he will have an abundance; bur from the one who does not have, even what he does have shall be taken away. 30 "Throw out the worthless slave into the outer darkness; in that place there will be weeping and gnashing of teeth.

Matthew 25: 24—30 (NASB)

Don't wait for six strong men to bring you to church.

5 For the living know that they will die, but the dead know nothing; they have no further reward , and even the memory of them is forgotten.

Ecclesiastes 9:5 (NIV)

17 It is not the dead who praise the LORD, those who go down to silence; 18it is we who extol the LORD, both now and forever more. Praise the LORD.

Psalm 115:17 (NIV)

Stop, drop and roll, does not work in hell.

24 "And they will go out and look upon the dead bodies of those

who rebelled against me; their worm will not die, nor will their fire be quenched, and they will be loathsome to all mankind."

Isaiah 66:24 (NIV)

48 Where " 'their worm does not die, and the fire is not quenched.' 49 Everyone will be salted with fire.

Mark 9: 48—49 (NIV)

Get right or get left.

31 "When the Son of Man comes in his glory, and all the angels with him, he will sit on his throne in heavenly glory. 32All the nations will be gathered before him, and he will separate the people one from another as a shepherd separates the sheep from the goats. 33 He will put the sheep on his right and the goats on his left. 34 "Then the King will say to those on his right, 'Come, you who are blessed by my Father; take your inheritance, the kingdom prepared for you since the creation of the world.

Matthew 25:31—34 (NIV)

You think it's hot here!

41 Then he will say to those on his left hand, 'You that are accursed, depart from me into the eternal fire prepared for the devil and his angels;

Matthew 25: 41 (NRSV)

Where will you be setting in eternity?

15 and anyone whose name was not found written in the book of life was thrown into the lake of fire.

Revelation 20:15 (NRSV)

At times majority means fools are on the same side.

5 But the LORD came down to look at the city and the tower the people were building. 6 "Look!" he said. "The people are united, and they all speak the same languages. After this, nothing they set out to do will be impossible for them! 7 Come, let's go down and confuse the people with different languages. Then they won't be able to understand each other." 8 In that way, the LORD scattered them all over the world, and they stopped building the city. 9 That is why the city was called Babel, because that is where the LORD confused the people with different languages. In this way he scattered them all over the world.

Genesis 11: 5—9 (NLT)

Knowledge speaks but wisdom listens.

10 "Be still, and know that I am God! I am exalted among the nations, I am exalted in the earth."

Psalm 46:10 (NRSV)

13 If one gives answer before hearing, it is folly and shame.

Proverbs 18: 13 (NRSV)

20 Listen to advice and accept instruction, that you may gain wisdom for the future.

Proverbs 19:20 (NRSV)

Worry

Worry is something God does not want us to do. Because it doesn't help, and it just makes you feel worse. If there is concern about something pray about it and ask the Lord to ease or take away your concern before it turns to worry.

Thought For The Day

Let's keep our minds on the Lord, and our worries will disappear.

Worry

Worry looks around, faith looks up.

19 And my God shall supply all your need according to His riches in glory by Christ Jesus.

Philippians 4:19 (NKJV)

Worry is interest paid on trouble before it's due.

22 Cast your burden on the LORD, And He shall sustain you; He shall never permit the righteous to be moved.

Psalm 55:22 (NKJV)

Worry is the dark room in which negatives are developed.

6 Be anxious for nothing, but in everything by prayer and supplication with thanksgiving let your requests be made known to God. 7 And the peace of God, which surpasses all comprehension, will guard your hearts and your minds in Christ Jesus.

Philippians 4: 6—7 (NASB)

6 Therefore humble yourselves under the mighty hand of God, that He may exalt you at the proper time, 7 casting all your anxiety on Him, because He cares for you.

1st Peter 5: 6—7 (NASB)

Three days a week God tells us not to worry, yesterday, today and tomorrow.

27 Who of you by worrying can add a single hour to his life?

28 "And why do you worry about clothes? See how the lilies of the field grow. They do not labor or spin. 29 Yet I tell you that not even Solomon in all his splendor was dressed like one of these. 30 If that is how God clothes the grass of the field, which is here today and tomorrow is thrown into the fire, will he not much more clothe

you, O you of little faith? 31 So do not worry, saying, 'What shall we eat?' or 'What shall we drink?' or 'What shall we wear?' 32 For the pagans run after all these things, and your heavenly Father knows that you need them. 33 But seek first his kingdom and his righteousness, and all these things will be given to you as well. 34 Therefore do not worry about tomorrow, for tomorrow will worry about itself. Each day has enough trouble of its own.

Matthew 6: 27—34 (NIV)

Don't be anxious about tomorrow, God is already there.

7 "Blessed is the man who trusts in the LORD, And whose hope is the LORD.

Jeremiah 17:7 (NKJV)

Worry is the waste of a good imagination.

25 Worry weighs a person down; an encouraging word cheers a person up.

Proverbs 12:25 (NLT)

29And do not keep striving for what you are to eat and what you are to drink, and do not keep worrying. 30For it is the nations of the world that strive after all these things, and your Father knows that you need them. 31Instead, strive for his kingdom, and these things will be given to you as well.

Luke 12: 29—31 (NRSV)

God's Love

God's love is unselfish just look around and see what He has given us. He has given us the sunshine, the stars, the rain, guidance, cleansing, and peace.

Who else could give us all of this unselfishly?

God's Love

I see God's love in the sunshine
I see God's love in the showers
I feel God's love surround me,
when I gaze at the evening stars.

God's love passes all understanding
It is full and complete.
Gives us peace and contentment,
and never will deplete.

God's love gives us guidance
along life's pathway,
and cleansing our hearts from all sin.
Thus making it possible that,
to heaven we may enter in.

So let us give God all the glory
and thank Him for His wonderful love.
For that peace, that passes all understanding
that comes from the throne above.

From my Stepfather
Homer Haley
Written—1980

We Cannot Work our way to God

It is easy to want to find a way to do something to earn our way to God. It doesn't seem fair. If I got myself into this mess, then I should be able to get out of it. But no good works will ever be enough to get to God.

5he saved us, not because of the righteous things we had done, but because of his mercy.

Titus 3:5a (NLT)

8God saved you by his grace when you believed. And you can't take credit for this; it is a gift from God. 9 Salvation is not a reward for the good things we have done, so none of us can boast about it.

Ephesians 2:8—9 (NLT)

Fluffy Clouds

The clouds are like fluffy cotton in the sky. Only God can create such things. Did you ever think how our Big Awesome God could create something so soft and gentle looking?

Fluffy Clouds

On a calm sunny day, we see fluffy white clouds,
slowly and lazily floating away.
Against the horizon we scan, Oh! What beauty,
created by the Master's hand.

Connie L. Parmenter

Help, Helper

At some time or another we all need help or a helper. So we need to pray and ask God for His help.

Thought For The Day

If we have Jesus in our hearts we have a helper for life.

Help / Helper

Are you at the end of your rope? Ask God for a knot.

17 Unless the LORD had been my help, My soul would soon have settled in silence.

Psalm 94:17 (NKJV)

12 Give us help from trouble, For the help of man is useless.

Psalm 108:12 (NKJV)

7 "For the Lord God will help Me; Therefore I will not be disgraced; Therefore I have set My face like a flint, And I know that I will not be ashamed. 9 Surely the Lord God will help Me; Who is he who will condemn Me?

Isaiah 50:7, 9a (NKJV)

13 No temptation has overtaken you except such as is common to man; but God is faithful, who will not allow you to be tempted beyond what you are able, but with the temptation will also make the way of escape, that you may be able to bear it.

1st Corinthians 10:13 (NKJV)

Jesus is a friend who walked in when the world walked out.

24 A man who has friends must himself be friendly, But there is a friend who sticks closer than a brother.

Proverbs 18: 24 (NKJV)

17 As iron sharpens iron, So a man sharpens the countenance of his friend.

Proverbs 27: 17 (NKJV)

Silence is often misinterpreted, never misquoted. 1 I said, "I will guard my ways That I may not sin with my tongue; I will guard my mouth as with a muzzle While the wicked are in my presence."

Psalm 39:1 (NASB)

23 He who guards his mouth and his tongue, Guards his soul from troubles.

Proverbs 21:23 (NASB)

A tongue weighs almost nothing, but few can hold it.

5 Likewise the tongue is a small part of the body, but it makes great boasts. Consider what a great forest is set on fire by a small spark. 6 The tongue also is a fire, a world of evil among the parts of the body. It corrupts the whole person, sets the whole course of his life on fire, and is itself set on fire by hell. 7 All kinds of animals, birds, reptiles and creatures of the sea are being tamed and have been tamed by man, 8 but no man can tame the tongue. It is a restless evil, full of deadly poison. 9 With the tongue we praise our Lord and Father, and with it we curse men, who have been made in God's likeness.

James 3: 5—9 (NIV)

In Christ you can thrive, not just survive.

3 Praise be to the God and Father of our Lord Jesus Christ, who has blessed us in the heavenly realms with every spiritual blessing in Christ.

Ephesians 1:3 (NIV)

4 But because of his great love for us, God, who is rich in mercy, 5 made us alive with Christ even when we were dead in transgressions—it is by grace you have been saved.

Ephesians 2: 4-5 (NIV)

17 so that Christ may dwell in your hearts through faith. And I pray that you, being rooted and established in love, 18 may have power, together with all the saints, to grasp how wide and long and high and deep is the love of Christ, 19 and to know this love that surpasses knowledge—that you may be filled to the measure of all the fullness of God. 20 Now to him who is able to do immeasurably more than all we ask or imagine, according to his power that is at work within us,

Ephesians 3:17-20 (NIV)

Can't sleep? Try counting your blessings.

10 Bring the full tithe into the storehouse, so that there may be food in my house, and thus put me to the test, says the LORD of hosts; see if I will not open the windows of heaven for you and pour down for you an overflowing blessing.

Malachi 3:10 (NRSV)

3 "Blessed are the poor in spirit, for theirs is the kingdom of heaven. 4 "Blessed are those who mourn, for they will be comforted. 5 "Blessed are the meek, for they will inherit the earth. 6 "Blessed are those who hunger and thirst for righteousness, for they will be filled. 7 "Blessed are the merciful, for they will receive mercy. 8 "Blessed are the pure in heart, for they will see God. 9 "Blessed are the peacemakers, for they will be called children of God. 10 "Blessed are those who are persecuted for righteousness' sake, for theirs is the kingdom of heaven. 11 "Blessed are you when people revile you and persecute you and utter all kinds of evil against you falsely on my account. 12 Rejoice and be glad, for your reward is great in heaven, for in the same way they persecuted the prophets who were before you.

Matthew 5: 3—12 (NRSV)

When you are down: look up for help.

1 I will lift up my eyes to the hills—From whence comes my help? 2 My help comes from the LORD, Who made heaven and earth.

Psalm 121: 1-2 (NKJV)

10 Fear not, for I am with you; Be not dismayed, for I am your God. I will strengthen you, yes, I will help you, I will uphold you with My righteous right hand.'

Isaiah 41:10 (NKJV)

For every burden, God lends a hand.

11 For I know the thoughts that I think toward you, says the LORD, thoughts of peace and not of evil, to give you a future and a hope.

Jeremiah 29: 11 (NKJV)

26 Then the word of the LORD came to Jeremiah, saying, 27 "Behold I am the LORD, the God of all flesh. Is there anything too hard for Me?

Jeremiah 32: 26—27 (NKJV)

There are some questions that can't be answered by Google.

3 'Call to Me, and I will answer you, and show you great and mighty things, which you do not know.'

Jeremiah 33:3 (NKJV)

11 For the Scripture says, "Whoever believes on Him will not be put to shame." 12 For there is no distinction between Jew and Greek, for the same Lord over all is rich to all who call upon

Him. 13 For "whoever calls on the name of the LORD shall be saved."

Romans 10: 11—13 (NKJV)

Give your troubles to God He's up all night anyway.

3 He will not allow your foot to slip; He who keeps you will not slumber. 4 Behold, He who keeps Israel Will neither slumber nor sleep.

Psalm 121: 3—4 (NASB)

Finger pointing, or hand lending?

17 But whoever has this world's goods, and sees his brother in need, and shuts up his heart from him, how does the love of God abide in him?

1st John 3:17 (NKJV)

Lord, keep your arm around my shoulder and your hand across my mouth.

29 Don't use foul or abusive language. Let everything you say be good and helpful, so that your words will be an encouragement to those who hear them.

Ephesians 4:29 (NLT)

26 If you claim to be religious but don't control your tongue, you are fooling yourself, and your religion is worthless. James 1:26 (NLT)

Lost? Come in for direction.

35 Jesus said to them, "I am the bread of life. Whoever comes to me will never be hungry, and whoever believes in me will never

be thirsty. 36 But I said to you that you have seen me and yet do not believe. 37 Everything that the Father gives me will come to me, and anyone who comes to me I will never drive away; 38 for I have come down from heaven, not to do my own will, but the will of him who sent me. 39 And this is the will of him who sent me, that I should lose nothing of all that he has given me, but raise it up on the last day. 40 This is indeed the will of my Father, that all who see the Son and believe in him may have eternal life; and I will raise them up on the last day."

John 6: 35—40 (NRSV)

Jesus never asks us to go through a valley He's never passed through.

13No temptation has overtaken you but such is common to man; and God is faithful, who will not allow you to be tempted beyond what you are able, but with the temptation will provide the way of escape also, so that you will be able to endure it.

1st Corinthians 10: 13 (NASB)

14 Since, then, we have a great high priest who has passed through the heavens, Jesus, the Son of God, let us hold fast to our confession. 15 For we do not have a high priest who is unable to sympathize with our weaknesses, but we have one who in every respect has been tested as we are, yet without sin. 16 Let us therefore approach the throne of grace with boldness, so that we may receive mercy and find grace to help in time of need.

Hebrews 4: 14—16 (NRSV)

What A Beautiful Night

As we see the night with snow, moon and rabbits.

Where does it all come from? Think about it.

What a Beautiful Night

What a beautiful night with the snow covered ground,
I looked out my window not making a sound.
The moon was shining ever so bright
I saw two rabbits, Oh! What a delight.
What could I say
it seemed the moon turned the night into day.
God! What a blessing it is,
your handy work to us you give.

Connie L. Parmenter

Love

We should love each other like God loves us. With no strings attached.

Thought For The Day

No one loves us more than God.

No one knows us better than God.

No one cares for us like God.

Love

God's purpose is greater than our problems.

8 But God demonstrates His own love toward us, in that while we were yet sinners, Christ died for us.

Romans 5:8 (NASB)

28 And we know that God causes all things to work together for good to those who love God, to those who are called according to His purpose.

Romans 8:28 (NASB)

Need a friend? Inquire within.

13 No one has greater love than this, to lay down one's life for one's friends. 14 You are my friends if you do what I command you. 15 I do not call you servants any longer, because the servant does not know what the master is doing; but I have called you friends, because I have made known to you everything that I have heard from my Father.

John 15:13—15 (NRSV)

Love is the very heart of God.

16 For God so loved the world that He gave His only begotten Son, that whoever believes in Him should not perish but have everlasting life.

John 3:16 (NKJV)

8 But God demonstrates His own love toward us, in that while we were still sinners, Christ died for us.

Romans 5:8 (NKJV)

He has everything in His hands, yet He still takes time for you.

28 "Come to Me, all who are weary and heavy laden, and I will give you rest. 29 "Take My yoke upon you and learn from Me, for I am gentle and humble in heart, and YOU WILL FIND REST FOR YOUR SOULS. 30 "For My yoke is easy and My burden is light."

Matthew 11:28—30 (NASB)

13for it is God who is at work in you, both to will and to work for His good pleasure.

Philippians 2:13 (NASB)

Trials can be God's way to triumphs.

12 Blessed is the man who endures temptation; for when he has been approved, he will receive the crown of life which the Lord has promised to those who love Him.

James 1:12 (NKJV)

Live God's love.

7 Beloved, let us love one another, for love is from God; and everyone who loves is born of God and knows God. 8 The one who does not love does not know God, for God is love. 9 By this the love of God was manifested in us, that God has sent His only begotten Son into the world so that we might live through Him. 10 In this is love, not that we loved God, but that He loved us and sent His Son to be the propitiation for our sins. 11 Beloved, if God so loved us, we also ought to love one another.

1st John 4: 7-11 (NASB)

Love is a blessed boomerang.

34 So now I am giving you a new commandment: Love each other. Just as I have loved you, you should love each other.

35 Your love for one another will prove to the world that you are my disciples."

John 13:34—35 (NLT)

14 Above all, clothe yourselves with love, which binds us together in perfect harmony.

Colossians 3:14 (NLT)

A little love can make a big difference.

10 Love does no harm to a neighbor; therefore love is the fulfillment of the law.

Romans 13: 10 (NKJV)

14 Let all that you do be done with love.

1st Corinthians 16:14 (NKJV)

If we offer God second place we offer Him nothing.

37 Jesus said to him, " 'You shall love the LORD your God with all your heart, with all your soul, and with all your mind.' 38 This is the first and great commandment. 39 and the second is like it: 'You shall love your neighbor as yourself.' 40 On these two commandments hang all the Law and the Prophets.

Matthew 22: 37—40 (NKJV)

Do unto others as if you were the others.

3 Do nothing from selfish ambition or conceit, but in humility

regard others as better than yourselves. ₄ Let each of you look not to your own interests, but to the interests of others.

Philippians 2: 3—4 (NRSV)

₁₂ "In everything, therefore, treat people the same way you want them to treat you, for this is the Law and the Prophets.

Matthew 7:12 (NASB)

A hug is an ideal gift. "One size fits all."

₁₆ Greet one another with a holy kiss. All the churches of Christ greet you.

Romans 16:16 (NRSV)

₁₉ We love because he first loved us.

1ˢᵗ John 4:19 (NRSV)

At every opportunity—do good.

₁₀ Therefore, whenever we have the opportunity, we should do good to everyone—especially to those in the family of faith.

Galatians 6:10 (NLT)

No one is beyond God's love.

₉ "As the Father loved Me, I also have loved you; abide in My love.

John 15:9 (NKJV)

God's timing is perfect even in death.

₈ But God proves his love for us in that while we still were sinners Christ died for us.

Romans 5:8 (NRSV)

Be an organ donor—give your heart to Jesus.

37 Jesus said to him, " 'You shall love the LORD your God with all your heart, with all your soul, and with all your mind.'

Matthew 22: 37 (NKJV)

The world uses duct tape to fix everything, Jesus used nails.

14 erasing the record that stood against us with its legal demands. He set this aside, nailing it to the cross.

Colossians 2: 14 (NRSV)

18 There they crucified him, and with him two others, one on either side, with Jesus between them.

John 19:18 (NRSV)

Give God your all, and there's nothing left for the devil.

5 And you must love the LORD God with all your heart, all your soul, and all your strength.

Deuteronomy 6:5 (NLT)

That: "Love your neighbor" thing. I meant that! God

9 For the commandments, "You shall not commit adultery," "You shall not murder," "You shall not steal," "You shall not bear false witness," "You shall not covet," and if there is any other commandment, are all summed up in this saying, namely, "You shall love your neighbor as yourself." 10 Love does no harm to a neighbor; therefore love is the fulfillment of the law.

Romans 13: 9—10 (NKJV)

One proof of your love is how you handle reproof.

18 He who ignores discipline comes to poverty and shame, but whoever heeds correction is honored.

Proverbs 13:18 (NIV)

5 A fool spurns his father's discipline, but whoever heeds correction shows prudence.

Proverbs 15: 5 (NIV)

We may overlook God, but He always looks out for us.

16 "For God so loved the world that he gave his one and only Son, that whoever believes in him shall not perish but have eternal life.

John 3: 16 (NIV)

You and God make a majority.

31What, then, shall we say in response to this? If God is for us, who can be against us?

Romans 8: 31 (NIV)

It's hard to look down on people when looking up to God.

31Do unto others as you would like them to do to you.

Luke 6: 31 (NLT)

8Most important of all, continue to show deep love for each other, for love covers a multitude of sins.

1st Peter 4: 8 (NLT)

Christmas

Christmas is a time we celebrate the birth of Christ.

Without Christ there would be no———————-mas.

Think about it!

Christmas

Christmas comes but once a year,
this day many folks hold dear.
Because it was on this morn,
that the little Christ child was born.
The shepherds from the fields did come,
to see the Savior of whom the angles sung.
For in a manger He was laid long ago,
let us all spread the Good News, for everyone should know.

Connie L. Parmenter

Jesus, Christ

God's one and only Son who died on a cross for us. What a Savior! Invite Him into your heart today.

Thought For The Day

Remember He died for us, so the least we can do is to invite Him into our hearts and to live for Him.

Jesus / Christ

No Jesus, no peace. Know Jesus, know peace.

33 I have told you all this so that you may have peace in me. Here on earth you will have many trials and sorrows. But take heart, because I have overcome the world."

John 16:33 (NLT)

14 For Christ himself has brought peace to us. He united Jews and Gentiles into one people when, in his own body on the cross, he broke down the wall of hostility that separated us.

Ephesians 2:14 (NLT)

Hungry; Soul food served here.

32 Then Jesus said to them, "Most assuredly, I say to you, Moses did not give you the bread from heaven, but My Father gives you the true bread from heaven. 33 For the bread of God is He who comes down from heaven and gives life to the world." 34 Then they said to Him, 'Lord, give us this bread always." 35 And Jesus said to them, " I am the bread of life. He who comes to Me shall never hunger, and he who believes in Me shall never thirst."

John 6:32—35 (NKJV)

48 I am the bread of life. 49 Your fathers ate the manna in the wilderness, and are dead. 50 This is the bread which comes down from heaven, that one may eat of it and not die. 51 I am the living bread which came down from heaven. If anyone eats of this bread, he will live forever; and the bread that I shall give is My flesh, which I shall give for the life of the world."

John 6:48—51 (NKJV)

The greatest gift of all: "Jesus."

11 Today in the town of David a Savior has been born to you; he is Christ the Lord.

Luke 2:11 (NIV)

Redemption equals God's perfect gift.

22 even the righteousness of God, through faith in Jesus Christ, to all and on all who believe. For there is no difference; 23 for all have sinned and fall short of the glory of God, 24 being justified freely by His grace through the redemption that is in Christ Jesus,

Romans 3: 22—24 (NKJV)

The task ahead of us is never as great as the power behind us.

18 And Jesus came and spoke to them, saying, "All authority has been given to Me in heaven and on earth. 19 Go therefore and make disciples of all the nations, baptizing them in the name of the Father and of the Son and of the Holy Spirit, 20 teaching them to observe all things that I have commanded you; and lo, I am with you always, even to the end of the age." Amen

Matthew 28: 18—20 (NKJV)

13 I can do all things through Christ who strengthens me.

Philippians 4: 13 (NKJV)

Everybody is somebody and Jesus is Lord.

18 And he is the head of the body, the church; he is the beginning and the firstborn from among the dead, so that in everything he

might have the supremacy. 19 For God was pleased to have all his fullness dwell in him,

Colossians 1:18—19 (NIV)

Without Christ, there wouldn't be a Christmas.

11 for today in the city of David there has been born for you a Savior, who is Christ the Lord.

Luke 2:11 (NASB)

6 For a child will be born to us, a son will be given to us; And the government will rest on His shoulders; And His name will be called Wonderful Counselor, Mighty God, Eternal Father, Prince of Peace.

Isaiah 9:6 (NASB)

In deep water; Trust the one who can walk on water.

25 And early in the morning he came walking toward them on the sea. 26 But when the disciples saw him walking on the sea, they were terrified, saying, "It is a ghost!" And they cried out in fear. 27 But immediately Jesus spoke to them and said, "Take heart, it is I; do not be afraid." 28 Peter answered him, "Lord, if it is you, command me to come to you on the water." 29 He said, "Come." So Peter got out of the boat, started walking on the water, and came toward Jesus. 30 But when he noticed the strong wind, he became frightened, and beginning to sink, he cried out, "Lord, save me!" 31 Jesus immediately reached out his hand and caught him, saying to him, "You of little faith, why did you doubt?"

Matthew 14: 25—31 (NRSV)

The key to heaven was hung high on a nail.

18 There they crucified him, and with him two others, one on either side, with Jesus between them.

John 19:18 (NRSV)

Life without Jesus is like a pencil without a point, worthless.

66 From that time many of His disciples went back and walked with Him no more. 67 Then Jesus said to the twelve, "Do you also want to go away?" 68 But Simon Peter answered Him, "Lord, to whom shall we go? You have the words of eternal life. 69 Also we have come to believe and know You are the Christ, the Son of the living God."

John 6: 66—69 (NKJV)

11 And this is the testimony: God gave us eternal life, and this life is in his Son. 12 Whoever has the Son has life; whoever does not have the Son of God does not have life. 13 I write these things to you who believe in the name of the Son of God, so that you may know that you have eternal life.

1ˢᵗ John 5:11—13 (NRSV)

Our power and light comes from the Son.

20 For the kingdom of God is not in word but in power.

1ˢᵗ Corinthians 4:20 (NKJV)

13I can do all things through him who strengthens me.

Philippians 4: 13 (NRSV)

God

What can I say about God? He is awesome, He is everywhere and He made us all. And He can save us all for eternity.

God

Is God real? How do you feel? Or
Is God fake? What do you think?
No one has ever seen God tis true,
but look around and see what He has given to you.

Flowers of all different colors and birds that sing so sweet,
the rainbow after a rain and a high mountain peak.
The fluffy white clouds that float gently by,
and the streaked lighting, that lights up the sky.

On those warm summer days when you're out having fun
remember, it is God who gave you the sun.
And to cool you He gave you a gentle breeze
and the shade from the giant oak trees.

More than these things for you He has done
for He has given to you Jesus His one and only Son.
For your sins He died in your place
for He is the only way to heaven,
thanks to God's amazing grace.

Connie L. Parmenter

God has a Solution

Since we cannot do anything to earn our way to God, He loved us so much that He provided a way that we can live with Him.

8But God demonstrates his own love for us in this: While we were still sinners, Christ died for us.

Romans 5:8 (NIV)

25He was handed over to die because of our sins, and he was raised to life to make us right with God.

Romans 4:25 (NLT)

16"For God loved the world so much that he gave his one and only Son, so that everyone who believes in him will not parish but have eternal life.

John 3:16 (NLT)

The important part to remember, though, is that there is only one solution. We cannot add anything to it or find a way around it.

6Jesus told him, "I am the way, the truth, and the life. No one comes to the Father except through me. John 14:6

Forgiveness, Grace

We need to forgive others for any wrong they do to us. For this is what God wants for us to do.

Thought For The Day

No matter what problems we have, no matter how bad things may seem. God tells us that His grace is all we need.

Forgiveness / Grace

You are not too bad to come in. You are not too bad to stay out.

16 "For God loved the world so much that he gave his one and only Son, so that everyone who believes in him will not perish but have eternal life. 17 God sent his Son into the world not to judge the world, but to save the world through him. 18 "There is no judgment against anyone who believes in him. But anyone who does not believe in him has already been judged for not believing in God's one and only Son.

John 3: 16—18 (NLT)

God can break us and only He can remake us.

17 This means that anyone who belongs to Christ has become a new person. The old life is gone; a new life has begun!

2nd Corinthians 5:17 (NLT)

10 Put on your new nature, and be renewed as you learn to know your Creator and become like him.

Colossians 3:10 (NLT)

If your request is denied, God's grace is supplied.

9 And He said to me, "My grace is sufficient for you, for My strength is made perfect in weakness." Therefore most gladly I will rather boast in my infirmities, that the power of Christ may rest upon me.

2nd Corinthians 12:9 (NKJV)

31 But those who wait on the LORD Shall renew their strength; They shall mount up with wings like eagles, They shall run and not be weary, They shall walk and not faint.

Isaiah 40:31 (NKJV)

Kindness is always in season.

17 A kind man benefits himself, but a cruel man brings himself harm.

Proverbs 11:17 (NIV)

32 Be kind and compassionate to one another, forgiving each other, just as in Christ God forgave you.

Ephesians 4: 32 (NKJV)

Enemies are best destroyed by turning them into friends.

7 When a man's ways please the LORD, He makes even his enemies to be at peace with him.

Proverbs 16:7 (NKJV)

God is the greatest teacher of forgiveness.

25 "I, even I, am he who blots out your transgressions, for my own sake, and remembers your sins no more.

Isaiah 43:25 (NIV)

1 Therefore, there is now no condemnation for those who are in Christ Jesus,

Romans 8:1 (NIV)

32 Be kind and compassionate to one another, forgiving each other, just as in Christ God forgave you.

Ephesians 4: 32 (NIV)

An unforgiving person always keeps score.

12 as far as the east is from the west, so far has he removed our transgressions from us.

Psalm 103:12 (NIV)

3 So watch yourselves. "If your brother sins, rebuke him, and if he repents, forgive him. 4 If he sins against you seven times in a day, and seven times comes back to you and says, 'I repent,' forgive him."

Luke 17: 3—4 (NIV)

Morally bankrupt? God offers instant credit.

7 so that, having been justified by his grace, we might become heirs having the hope of eternal life.

Titus 3:7 (NIV)

3 The Son is the radiance of God's glory and the exact representation of his being, sustaining all things by his powerful word.

Hebrews 1:3a (NIV)

There is no right time to do a wrong thing.

14 " If you forgive others who sin against you, your heavenly Father will forgive you. 15 But if you refuse to forgive others, your heavenly Father will not forgive your sins.

Matthew 6: 14—15 (NLT)

You cannot know the resources of God, until you attempt an impossible task.

9 but he said to me, "My grace is sufficient for you, for power is made perfect in weakness." So, I will boast all the more gladly of my weakness, so the power of Christ may dwell in me.

2nd Corinthians 12: 9 (NRSV)

All Around The Town

On a cold winter night take a tour around your town and feel the crisp air. See how the frost has gathered on the roofs. But if you wait until late the next day it may be gone.

All Around the Town

All around the town on a cold winter's night
you can see the smoke rising from chimneys,
with the moon ever so bright.
The roofs are white where the frost does lay,
but disappears by late in the day.
The air is crisp, cause the wind does blow,
and you know the Lord is near as He causes
it to be so.

Connie L. Parmenter

Truth

The truth is reliable and trustworthy, and can build a person up, but a lie brings a person down and is harmful to all.

Thought For The Day

Make sure we always tell the truth, so our testimony will show the love of God.

It's better to stand alone in the truth then together in a lie.

22 Then Elijah said to the people, "I alone am left a prophet of the LORD, but Baal's prophets are 450 men. 36 At the time of the offering of the evening sacrifice, Elijah the prophet came near and said, "O LORD, the God of Abraham, Isaac and Israel, today let it be known that You are God in Israel and that I am Your servant and I have done all these things at Your word.

37 "Answer me, O LORD, answer me, that this people may know that You, O LORD, are God, and that You have turned their heart back again." 38 Then the fire of the LORD fell and consumed the burnt offering and the wood and the stones and the dust, and licked up the water that was in the trench. 39 When all the people saw it, they fell on their faces; and they said, "The LORD, He is God; the LORD, He is God."

1st Kings 18:22, 36—39 (NASB)

5 we did not submit to them even for a moment, so that the truth of the gospel might always remain with you.

Galatians 2:5 (NRSV)

We cannot worship one we do not know.

10 Be still and know that I am God; I will be exalted among the nations, I will be exalted in the earth!

Psalm 46:10 (NKJV)

3 Know that the LORD, He is God; It is He who has made us, and not we ourselves; We are His people and the sheep of His pasture.

Psalm 100:3 (NKJV)

Your name is on God's calendar

29 For God knew his people in advance, and he chose them to become like his Son, so that his Son would be the firstborn among many brothers and sisters. 30 And having chosen them, he called them to come to him. And having called them, he gave them right standing with himself. And having given them, right standing, he gave them his glory. 31 What shall we say about such wonderful things as these? If God is for us, who can ever be against us?

Romans 8: 29—31 (NLT)

No problem is too big for God's power. No person too small for God's love.

34 Then Peter began to speak to them: "I truly understand that God shows no partiality, 35 but in every nation anyone who fears him and does what is right is acceptable to him.

Acts 10:34—35 (NRSV)

With God there are no endings only endless beginnings.

1 In the beginning God created the heavens and the earth.

Genesis 1:1 (NLT)

1 In the beginning the Word already existed. The Word was with God, and the Word was God. 2 He existed in the beginning with God.

John 1: 1—2 (NLT)

Need a family? We adopt.

4 But when the right time came, God sent his Son, born of a woman, subject to the law. 5 God sent him to buy freedom for us who were slaves to the law, so that he could adopt us as his very

own children. 6 And because we are his children, God has sent the Spirit of his Son into the hearts, prompting us to call out, "Abba Father." 7 Now you are no longer a slave but God's own child. And since you are his child, God has made you his heir.

Galatians 4: 4—7 (NLT)

Will the road you're on get you to my place? God!

31 Then Jesus said to those Jews who believed Him, "If you abide in My word, you are My disciples indeed. 32 And you shall know the truth, and the truth shall make you free."

John 8:31—32 (NKJV)

6 Jesus said, "I am the way, the truth, and the life. No one comes to the Father except through Me.

John 14:6 (NKJV)

We don't need more to be thankful, we need to be more thankful.

11 I am not saying this because I am in need, for I have learned to be content whatever the circumstances. 12 I know what it is to be in need, and I know what it is to have plenty. I have learned the secret of being content in any and every situation, weather well fed or hungry, weather living in plenty or in want. 13 I can do everything through him who gives me strength.

Philippians 4: 11—13 (NIV)

Wise men seek Him.

17 "I love those who love me; And those who diligently seek me will find me.

Proverbs 8: 17 (NASB)

1 Now after Jesus was born in Bethlehem of Judea in the days of Herod the king, magi from the east arrived in Jerusalem, saying, 2 "Where is He who has been born King of the Jews? For we saw His star in the east and have come to worship Him."

Matthew 2:1—2 (NASB)

When you have the source of power, you have power over sin.

16 For I am not ashamed of this Good News about Christ. It is the power of God at work, saving everyone who believes—the Jew first and also the Gentile.

Romans 1:16 (NLT)

10 A final word: Be strong in the Lord and in his mighty power.

Ephesians 6:10 (NLT)

3 By his divine power, God has given us everything we need for a godly life. We have received all of this by coming to know him, the one who called us to himself by means of his marvelous glory and excellence.

2nd Peter 1:3 (NLT)

Many books can inform, only the Bible can transform.

15 Be diligent to present yourself approved to God, a worker who does not need to be ashamed, rightly dividing the word of truth.

2nd Timothy 2:15 (NKJV)

16 All scripture is given by inspiration of God, and is profitable for doctrine, for reproof, for correction, for instruction in righteousness, 17 that the man of God may be complete, thoroughly equipped for every good work.

2nd Timothy 3:16—17 (NKJV)

Are you searching for the truth? Read the Bible.

16 They are not of the world, just as I am not of the world.

17 Sanctify them by Your truth. Your word is truth.

John 17: 16—17 (NKJV)

In God's house on Sunday: God in your house everyday.

11 For I know the plans I have for you," declares the LORD, "plans to prosper you and not to harm you, plans to gives you hope and a future.

Jeremiah 29: 11 (NIV)

13 No temptation has overtaken you except such as is common to man; but God is faithful, who will not allow you to be tempted beyond what you are able, but with the temptation will also make the way of escape, that you may be able to bear it.

1ˢᵗ Corinthians 10:13 (NKJV)

Dusty Bibles lead to dirty lives.

15 Do your best to present yourself to God as one approved by him, a worker who has no need to be ashamed, rightly explaining the word of truth.

2ⁿᵈ Timothy 2: 15 (NRSV)

The Ghost here is Holy.

26 "But the Helper, the Holy Spirit, whom the Father will send in My name, He will teach you all things, and bring to your remembrance all that I said to you.

John 14: 26 (NASB)

8 But you will receive power when the Holy Spirit has come upon you; and you will be my witnesses in Jerusalem, in all Judea and Samaria, and to the ends of the earth."

Acts 1: 8 (NRSV)

Example is language everyone understands.

15 I have set you an example that you should do as I have done for you.

John 13:15 (NIV)

21 To this you were called, because Christ suffered for you, leaving you an example, that you should follow in his steps.

1st Peter 2: 21 (NIV)

Sunsets equal a gift from God.

8 Those living far away fear your wonders; where morning dawns and evening fades.

Psalm 65:8 (NIV)

19 The moon marks off the seasons, and the sun knows when to go down.

Psalm 104: 19 (NIV)

God can do anything, but fail.

37 "For nothing will be impossible with God."

Luke 1:37 (NASB)

26 And looking at them Jesus said to them, "With people this is impossible, but with God all things are possible."

Matthew 19: 26 (NASB)

Behold the beauty of God's earth.

31 God saw all that He had made, and behold, it was very good. And there was evening and there was morning, the sixth day.

Genesis 1: 31 (NASB)

1 The heavens are telling of the glory of God; And their expanse is declaring the work of His hands.

Psalm 19: 1 (NASB)

God is in the business of fixing broken lives.

18 The LORD is near to the brokenhearted, and saves the crushed in spirit.

Psalm 34: 18 (NRSV)

10 Create in me a clean heart, O God, and put a new and right spirit within me. 11 Do not cast me away from your presence, and do not take your holy spirit from me. 12 Restore to me the joy of your salvation, and sustain in me a willing spirit.

Psalm 51: 10—12 (NRSV)

The Bible: more up—to date than tomorrow's newspaper.

160 The entirety of Your word is truth, and every one of Your righteous judgments endures forever.

Psalms119: 160 (NKJV)

Let Us Pause

In our busy lives with all the sights, sounds, in our happy times, our sad times, and even in all our troubles, yes we need to pause and thank God for all we have.

Let Us Pause

Let us pause to give thanks to the One up above,
who continually sends down to us His sweet love.
We deserve it not, as we well know,
but unto us the Lord does bestow.

Blessings upon blessings how they do mount,
so let us give thanks to God as them we do count.
Let us pause and reflect His love to us so dear,
love we should not neglect, but to Him show reverence and fear.

Connie L. Parmenter

Obey, Obedience

We are to obey, not only God but we should also obey our parents and those who are in authority over us. If it is not against God will.

Thought For The Day

Obedience should be a high priority for each one of us. Think about it and, think about the consequences of not obeying.

Obey / Obedience

Been taken for granted? Imagine how God feels.

8 Being found in appearance as a man, He humbled Himself by becoming obedient to the point of death, even death on the cross.

Philippians 2:8 (NASB)

7 During the days of Jesus' life on earth, he offered up prayers and petitions with loud cries and tears to the one who could save him from death, and he was heard because of his reverent submission. 8 Although he was a son, he learned obedience from what he suffered 9 and, once made perfect, he became the source of eternal salvation for all who obey him

Hebrews 5: 7—9 (NIV)

Jesus break our hearts, for what breaks yours.

36 Seeing the people, He felt compassion for them, because they were distressed and dispirited like sheep without a shepherd.

Matthew 9: 36 (NASB)

34 When Jesus went ashore, He saw a large crowd, and He felt compassion for them because they were like sheep without a shepherd; and He began to teach them many things.

Mark 6: 34 (NASB)

Let us be silent, that way we may hear the whisper of God.

12 After the earthquake came a fire, but the LORD was not in the fire. And after the fire came a gentle whisper.

1st Kings 19:12 (NIV)

14 "Listen to this, O Job; Stand still and consider the wondrous works of God.

Job 37: 14 (NKJV)

10 Be still and know that I am God; I will be exalted among the nations, I will be exalted in the earth!

Psalm 46: 10 (NKJV)

Don't put a question mark where God has put a period.

10 Obey the LORD your God and follow his commands and decrees that I give you today."

Deuteronomy 27: 10 (NIV)

29 But Peter and the apostles answered, "We must obey God rather than man.

Acts 5: 29 (NASB)

Led by the Spirit and living by the word.

25 Since we live by the Spirit, let us keep in step with the Spirit.

Galatians 5:25 (NIV)

13 We know that we live in him and he in us, because he has given us of his Spirit.

1st John 4: 13 (NIV)

The wise men followed the star, and then they followed the Son.

9 When they heard the king, they departed; and behold, the star which they had seen in the East went before them, till it came and stood over where the young Child was. 10 When they saw the

star, they rejoiced with exceedingly great joy. 11 And when they had come into the house, they saw the young Child with Mary His mother, and fell down and worshiped Him. And when they had opened their treasurers, they presented gifts to Him; gold, frankincense, and myrrh. 12Then, being divinely warned in a dream that they should not return to Herod, they departed for their own country another way.

Matthew 2: 9—12 (NKJV)

The Bible is God's prescription for the health of your soul.

20My son, give attention to my words; Incline your ear to my sayings. 21Do not let them depart from your eyes; Keep them in the midst of your heart; 22For they are life to those who find them, and health to all their flesh. 23Keep your heart with all diligence, For out of it spring the issues of life.

Proverbs 4: 20—23 (NKJV)

The best vitamin for a Christian is B1.

14You are the light of the world. A city that is set on a hill cannot be hidden. 15Nor do they light a lamp and put it under a basket, but on a lamp stand, and it gives light to all who are in the house. 16Let your light so shine before men, that they may see your good works and glorify your Father in heaven.

Matthew 5: 14—16 (NKJV)

15Therefore be careful how you walk, not as unwise men but as wise.

Ephesians 5: 15 (NASB)

Do the math, count your blessings.

20Now to Him who is able to do far more abundantly beyond all that we ask or think, according to the power that works within us,

Ephesians 3:20 (NASB)

1 "Now it shall be, if you diligently obey the LORD your God, being careful to do all His commandments which I command you today, the LORD your God will set you high above all the nations of the earth. 2 "All these blessings will come upon you and overtake you if you obey the LORD your God:

Deuteronomy 28:1—2 (NASB)

People who walk with God will always get to their destination.

28 "Come to Me, all who are weary and heavy laden, and I will give you rest. 29 "Take My yoke upon you and learn from Me, for I am gentle in heart, and YOU WILL FIND REST FOR YOUR SOULS. 30 "For My yoke is easy and My burden is light."

Matthew 11: 28—30 (NASB)

30 "And then the sign of the Son of Man will appear in the sky, and then all the tribes of the earth will morn, and they will see the SON OF MAN COMING ON THE CLOUDS OF THE SKY with power and great glory. 31 "And He will send forth His angels with a GREAT TRUMPET and THEY WILL GATHER TOGETHER His elect from the four winds, from one end of the sky to the other.

Matthew 24: 30—31 (NASB)

Make your eternal reservations now.

23Jesus answered him, "Those who love me will keep my word, and my Father will love them, and we will come to them and make our home with them.

John 14: 23 (NRSV)

Even Jesus had a fish story.

17Then Jesus said to them, "Follow Me, and I will make you become fishers of men."

Mark 1:17 (NKJV)

What's missing in ch—ch? Ur.

20For where two or three come together in my name, there am I with them"

Matthew 18: 20 (NIV)

25Not forsaking the assembling of ourselves together, as is the manner of some, but exhorting one another, and so much the more as you see the Day approaching.

Hebrews 10: 25 (NKJV)

You fish, God cleans.

18One day as Jesus was walking along the shore of the Sea of Galilee, he saw two brothers—Simon, also called Peter, and Andrew—throwing a net into the water, for they fished for a living. 19Jesus called out to them, "Come, follow me, and I will show you how to fish for people!" 20And they left their nets at once and followed him.

Matthew 4: 18—20 (NLT)

17This means that anyone who belongs to Christ has become a new person. The old life is gone; a new life has begun!

2nd Corinthians 5: 17 (NLT)

The best exercise is walking with God.

16For I command you this day to love the LORD your God and keep his commands, decrees, and regulations by walking in his ways. If you do this, you will live and multiply, and the LORD your God will bless you and the land you are about to enter and occupy.

Deuteronomy 30: 16 (NLT)

7 "This is what the LORD of Heaven's Armies says: If you follow my ways and carefully serve me, then you will be given authority over my Temple and its courtyard. I will let you walk among these standing here.

Zechariah 3: 7 (NLT)

Jesus—stand for Him now, He will stand for you later.

34He called the crowd with his disciples, and said to them, "If any want to become my followers, let them deny themselves and take up their cross and follow me. 35For those who want to save their life will lose it, and those who lose their life for my sake, and for the sake of the gospel, will save it. 36For what will it profit them to gain the whole world and forfeit their life? 37Indeed, what can they give in return for their life? 38Those who are ashamed of me and of my words in this adulterous and sinful generation, of them the Son of Man will also be ashamed when he comes in this glory of his Father with the holy angels."

Mark 8: 34—38 (NRSV)

Happiness is a path not a destination.

16Better is a little with the fear of the LORD, Than great treasure with trouble.

Proverbs 15: 16 (NKJV)

12I know that nothing is better for them than to rejoice, and to do good in their lives,

Ecclesiastes 3: 12 (NKJV)

Growing with God is a daily event.

17Therefore, dear friends, since you already know this, be on your guard so that you may not be carried away by the error of lawless men and fall from your secure position. 18But grow in the grace and knowledge of our Lord and Savior Jesus Christ. To him be glory both now and forever! Amen.

2nd Peter 3: 17—18 (NIV)

15Be diligent to present yourself approved to God, a worker who does not need to be ashamed, rightly dividing the word of truth.

2nd Timothy 2: 15 (NKJV)

Home improvement; take your family to church.

18 "You shall therefore impress these words of mine on your heart and on your soul; and you shall bind them as a sign on your hand, and they shall be as frontals on your forehead. 19 "You shall teach them to your sons, talking of them when you sit in your house and when you walk along the road and when you lie down and when you rise up. 20 "You shall write them on the doorposts of your house and on your gates,

Deuteronomy 11: 18—20 (NASB)

6Train up a child in the way he should go, Even when he is old he will not depart from it.

Proverbs 22: 6 (NASB)

If you only sample the Bible, you will never acquire a taste for it.

16 "Search from the book of the LORD, and read: Not one of these shall fail; Not one shall lack her mate. For My mouth has commanded it, and His Spirit has gathered them.

Isaiah 34: 16 (NKJV)

16Then those who feared the LORD spoke to one another, And the LORD listened and heard them; So a book of remembrance was written before Him For those who fear the LORD And who meditate on His name.

Malachi 3; 16 (NKJV)

8Finally, brethren, whatever things are true, whatever things are noble, whatever things are just, whatever things are pure, whatever things are lovely, whatever things are of good report, if there is any virtue and if there is anything praiseworthy—meditate on these things. 9The things which you learned and received and heard and saw in me, these do, and the God of peace will be with you.

Philippians 4: 8—9 (NKJV)

Growing with God is a daily event.

1Happy are those who do not follow the advice of the wicked, or take the path that sinners tread, or sit in the seat of scoffers; 2but their delight is in the law of the LORD, and on his law they meditate day and night.

Psalm 1: 1—2 (NRSV)

9For this reason, since the day we heard it, we have not ceased praying for you and asking that you may be filled with the knowledge of God's will in all spiritual wisdom and understanding, 10 so that you may lead lives worthy of the Lord, fully pleasing to him, as you bear fruit in every good work and as you grow in the knowledge of God.

Colossians 1: 9—10 (NRSV)

You can't hear if you don't listen.

20Listen to advice and accept instruction, that you may gain wisdom for the future.

Proverbs 19: 20 (NRSV)

19You must understand this, my beloved: let everyone be quick to listen, slow to speak, slow to anger;

James 1: 19 (NRSV)

Trust

If we trust God then we will want Him in our hearts and lives.

So what are you waiting for?

Ask Him into your heart today.

Trust

Happy is the person who
puts his trust in God.
He will ever be with them
where ever they trod.

He will never forsake them
He is a friend, and a guide.
He always will love us
Whatever be tide.

I am so glad I learned
to trust Him and I have
found His promises are true.
So walk with the Master
and skies will always be blue.

From my Stepfather
Homer Haley
Written—1980

Accept His Gift

Since Jesus is the only way to God, you need to do only one thing—accept Jesus' death as the replacement for the penalty of your sins. All you have to do is believe that His death is enough.

31**They replied, "Believe in the Lord Jesus and you will be saved,**

Acts 16: 31a (NLT)

9**If you confess with your mouth that Jesus is Lord and believe in your heart that God raised him from the dead, you will be saved.** 10**For it is by believing in your heart that you are made right with God, and it is by confessing with your mouth that you are saved.**

Romans 10: 9—10 (NLT)

Faith, Faithful

Faith is not questioning God's word, but reading and believing it.

Thought For The Day

Do we show our faith to others?

Are we faithful to God? We should be as He is faithful to us.

Faith / Faithful

It wasn't raining when Noah built the Ark.

7By faith Noah, warned by God about events as yet unseen, respected the warning and built an ark to save his household; by this he condemned the world and became an heir to the righteousness that is in accordance with faith.

Hebrews 11: 7 (NRSV)

God's vision, like faith sees beyond the impossible.

1Now faith is being sure of what we hope for and certain of what we do not see. Hebrews 11: 1 (NIV)

Faith is not only believing God can, it's knowing that He will.

12Because of Christ and our faith in him, we can now come boldly and confidently into God's presence.

Ephesians 3: 12 (NLT)

19and to know this love that surpasses knowledge—that you may be filled to the measure of all the fullness of God. 20Now to him who is able to do immeasurably more than all we ask or imagine, according to his power that is at work within us,

Ephesians 3: 19—20 (NIV)

Every saint has a past, every sinner has a future.

20Therefore no one will be declared righteous in his sight by observing the law; rather, through the law we become conscious of sin. 21But now a righteousness from God, apart from law, has been made known, to which the Law and the Prophets testify. 22This righteousness from God comes through faith in Jesus Christ to all who believe. There is no difference, 23for all have sinned and fall short of the glory of God, 24and are justified freely by his grace through the redemption that came by Jesus Christ. 25God presented him as a sacrifice of atonement, through faith in his blood. He did this to demonstrate his justice, because in his forbearance he had left the sins committed beforehand unpunished—26he did it to demonstrate his justice at the present time, so as to be just and the one who justifies the man who has faith in Jesus.

Romans 3: 20—26 (NIV)

Good enough…. isn't.

6But we are all like an unclean thing, And all our righteousness are like filthy rags; We all fade as a leaf, And our iniquities, like the wind, Have taken us away.

Isaiah 64: 6 (NKJV)

8For by grace you have been saved through faith, and that not of yourselves; it is the gift of God, 9not of works, lest anyone should boast.

Ephesians 2: 8—9 (NKJV)

The true measure of a person is what's in his heart.

33Sell your possessions and give to the poor. Provide purses for yourselves that will not wear out, a treasure in heaven that will not be exhausted, where no thief comes near and no moth destroys. 34For where your treasure is, there your heart will be also.

Luke 12: 33—34 (NIV)

19 "Do not store up for yourselves treasures on earth, where moth and rust destroy, and where thieves break in and steal. 20 "But store up for yourselves treasures in heaven, where neither moth

not rust destroys, and where thieves do not break in and steal; 21for where your treasure is, there your heart will be also.

Matthew 6: 19—21 (NASB)

Store the Bible in your heart not on a shelf.

8 This book of the law shall not depart out of your mouth; you shall meditate on it day and night, so that you may be careful to act in accordance with all that is written in it. For then you shall make your way prosperous, and then you shall be successful.

Joshua 1: 8 (NRSV)

11I treasure your word in my heart, so that I may not sin against you. Psalm 119: 11 (NRSV)

God grades on the cross, not the curve.

27Can we boast, then, that we have done anything to be accepted by God? No, because our acquittal is not based on obeying the law. It is based on faith. 28So we are made right with God through faith and not by obeying the law.

Romans 3: 27—28 (NLT)

6But if it is by grace, it is no longer on the basis of works, otherwise grace is no longer grace.

Romans 11:6 (NASB)

8For by grace you have been saved through faith; and that not of yourselves, it is a gift of God; 9not as a result of works, so that no one may boast.

Ephesians 2: 8—9 (NASB)

May your heart overflow, with Jesus this year.

19And my God will supply all your needs according to His riches in glory in Christ Jesus.

Philippians 4: 19 (NASB)

16Let us then approach the throne of grace with confidence, so that we may receive mercy and find grace to help us in our time of need.

Hebrews 4: 16 (NIV)

People see God every day, they just don't recognize Him.

20For ever since the world was created, people have seen the earth and sky. Through everything God made, they can clearly see his invisible qualities—his eternal power and divine nature. So they have no excuse for not knowing God.

Romans 1: 20 (NLT)

Read the Bible as if God were speaking to you, He is.

35Jesus heard that they had cast him out; and when He had found him, He said to him, "Do you believe in the Son of God?" 36He answered and said, "Who is He, Lord, that I may believe in Him?" 37And Jesus said to him, "You have both seen Him and it is He who is talking with you." 38Then he said, "Lord, I believe!" And he worshiped Him.

John 9: 35—38 (NKJV)

Faith honors God, God honors faith.

6And without faith it is impossible to please Him, for he who comes to God must believe that He is and that He is a rewarder of those who seek Him. 24By faith Moses, when he had grown up, refused to be called the son of Pharaoh's daughter, 25choosing rather to endure ill-treatment with the people of God than to enjoy the passing pleasures of sin, 26considering the reproach of Christ greater riches than the treasures of Egypt; for he was looking to the reward.

Hebrews 11: 6, 24—26 (NASB)

Evolution is a theory, not a fact.

26Then God said, "Let Us make man in Our image, according to Our likeness; let them have dominion over the fish of the sea, over the birds of the air, and over the cattle, over all the earth and over every creeping thing that creeps on the earth." 27So God created man in His own image; in the image of God He created him; male and female He created them.

Genesis 1: 26—27 (NKJV)

3For the time will come when men will not put up with sound doctrine. Instead, to suit their own desires, they will gather around them a great number of teachers to say what their itching ears want to hear. 4They will turn their ears away from the truth and turn aside to myths.

2nd Timothy 4: 3—4 (NIV)

No one has choked to death by swallowing their pride.

26Then Hezekiah repented of the pride of his heart, as did the people of Jerusalem; therefore the LORD'S wrath did not come upon them during the days of Hezekiah. 27Hezekiah had very great riches and honor, and he made treasuries for his silver and gold and for his precious stones, spices, shields and all kinds of valuables.

2nd Chronicles 32: 26—27 (NIV)

An obstacle is often a stepping stone.

2Consider it pure joy, my brothers, whenever you face trials of many kinds, 3because you know that the testing of your faith develops perseverance. 4Perseverance must finish its work so that you may be mature and complete, not lacking anything.

James 1: 2—4 (NIV)

Running low on faith? Stop in here and fill up.

16 " And on the basis of faith in His name, it is the name of Jesus which has strengthened this man whom you see and know; and the faith which comes through Him has given him this perfect health in the presence of you all.

Acts 3: 16 (NASB)

23 if indeed you continue in the faith firmly established and steadfast, and not moved away from the hope of the gospel that you have heard, which was proclaimed in all creation under heaven, and of which I, Paul, was made a minister.

Colossians 1: 23 (NASB)

Come in for a faith lift.

18 to open their eyes so that they may turn from darkness to light and from the dominion of Satan to God, that they may receive forgiveness of sins and an inheritance among those who have been sanctified by faith in Me.'

Acts 26: 18 (NASB)

2 in the hope of eternal life, which God, who cannot lie, promised long ages ago,

Titus 1: 2 (NASB)

It's amazing what can be done when no one cares who gets the credit.

23Whatever you do, work at it with all your heart, as working for the Lord, not for men,

Colossians 3: 23 (NIV)

An oak tree was once an acorn that stood its ground.

14For we have become partners of Christ, if only we hold our first confidence firm to the end.

Hebrews 3: 14 (NRSV)

Trust in God's timing.

1For everything there is a season, and a time for every matter under heaven:

Ecclesiastes 3: 1 (NRSV)

31but those who wait for the LORD shall renew their strength, they shall mount up with wings like eagles, they shall run and not be weary, they shall walk and not faint.

Isaiah 40: 31 (NRSV)

Walk with the Lord and you'll stay in step.

16So I say, live by the Spirit, and you will not gratify the desires of the sinful nature.

Galatians 5: 16 (NIV)

7But if we walk in the light, as he is in the light, we have fellowship with one another, and the blood of Jesus, his Son, purifies us from all sin.

1st John 1: 7 (NIV)

A Worn Bible usually belongs to someone who reads it.

8This Book of the Law shall not depart from your mouth, but you shall meditate in it day and night, that you may observe to do according to all that is written in it. For then you will make your way prosperous, and then you will have good success.

Joshua 1: 8 (NKJV)

13Hold fast the pattern of sound words which you have heard from me, in faith and love which are in Christ Jesus.

2nd Timothy 2: 13 (NKJV)

Feed your faith and fear will starve.

6Be anxious for nothing, but in everything by prayer and supplication with thanksgiving let your requests be made known to God.

Philippians 4: 6 (NASB)

7For God has not given us a spirit of timidity, but of power and love and discipline.

2nd Timothy 1: 7 (NASB)

WWJD = Walk with Jesus daily.

5For all the peoples walk, each in the name of its god, but we will walk in the name of the LORD our God forever and ever.

Micah 4: 5 (NRSV)

12I will make them strong in the LORD, and they shall walk in his name, says the LORD.

Zechariah 10: 12 (NRSV)

My soul finds rest in God alone.

14He said, "My presence will go with you, and I will give you rest."

Exodus 33: 14 (NRSV)

28 "Come to me, all you that are weary and are carrying heavy burdens, and I will give you rest.

Matthew 11: 28 (NRSV)

October Harvest

It only takes a few seeds planted in the ground and the sun and rain from God to make them grow into plants. Then soon there will be corn stalks towering up from the ground with ears full of corn. And the bean plants with pods full of beans. The farmer knows just the right time to harvest them.

October Harvest

Spring and summer has come and gone,
October is here and fall has begun.
From very early in the morn,
farmers are harvesting there beans and corn.
Till very late at night,
with the help of the harvest moon light.
Now they praise God for abundant yields,
then in the spring they'll plant new fields.

Connie L. Parmenter

Trust

If we trust God we will put our confidence in Him.

Thought For The Day

If we want to be trusted we also need to be trustworthy.

Trust

F.R.O.G. = Fully relying on God

1To you, O LORD, I lift up my soul.

Psalm 25: 1 (NRSV)

1Those who trust in the LORD are like Mount Zion, which cannot be moved, but abides forever.

Psalm 125: 1 (NRSV)

8Let me hear of your steadfast love in the morning, for in you I put my trust. Teach me the way I should go, for to you I lift up my soul.

Psalm 143: 8 (NRSV)

31What then are we to say about these things? If God is for us, who is against us?

Romans 8: 31 (NRSV)

Don't know God? Read the Bible.

1God is our refuge and strength, a very present help in trouble.

10 "Be still, and know that I am God! I am exalted among the nations, I am exalted in the earth."

Psalm 46: 1, 10 (NRSV)

3Know that the LORD, He is God; It is He who made us, and not we ourselves; We are His people and the sheep of His pasture.

Psalm 100: 3 (NKJV)

10For we are His workmanship, created in Christ Jesus for good works, which God prepared beforehand that we should walk in them.

Ephesians 2: 10 (NKJV)

Trust God's authority not man's majority.

7But the LORD said to Samuel, "Do not look at his appearance or at the height of his stature, because I have rejected him; for God sees not as man sees, for man looks at the outward appearance, but the LORD looks at the heart."

1st Samuel 16:7 (NASB)

4 "Where were you when I laid the foundation of the earth? Tell me, if you have understanding.

Job 38: 4 (NASB)

At the end of your rope is God and hope.

5Trust in the LORD with all your heart And do not lean on your own understanding. 6In all your ways acknowledge Him, And He will make your paths straight.

Proverbs 3: 5—6 (NASB)

6But Christ, as the Son, is in charge of God's entire house. And we are God's house, if we keep our courage and remain confident in our hope in Christ.

Hebrews 3: 6 (NLT)

18So God has given both his promise and his oath. These two things are unchangeable because it is impossible for God to lie. Therefore, we who have fled to him for refuse can have great confidence as we hold to the hope that lies before us. 19This hope is a strong and trustworthy anchor for our souls. It leads us through the curtain into God's inner sanctuary.

Hebrews 6: 18—19 (NLT)

Leaves change but God's love does not.

8Jesus Christ is the same yesterday, today, and forever.

Hebrews 13: 8 (NKJV)

12AND LIKE A MANTLE YOU WILL ROLL THEM UP; LIKE A GARMENT THEY WILL ALSO BE CHANGED. BUT YOU ARE THE SAME, AND YOUR YEARS WILL NOT COME TO AN END."

Hebrews 1:12 (NASB)

Give thanks for simple things.

18 in everything give thanks; for this is the will of God in Christ Jesus for you.

1st Thessalonians 5: 18 (NKJV)

If you don't enjoy what you have, how could you be happy with more?

5Let your conduct be without covetousness; be content with such things as you have. For He Himself has said, "I will never leave you nor forsake you."

Hebrews 13: 5 (NKJV)

God is the original recycler.

1Therefore I urge you, brethren, by the mercies of God, to present your bodies a living and holy sacrifice, acceptable to God, which is your spiritual service of worship. 2And do not be conformed to this world, but be transformed by the renewing of your mind, so that you may prove what the will of God is, that which is good and acceptable and perfect.

Romans 12: 1—2 (NASB)

Those who put God first will be happy at last.

₁ "Don't let your heart be troubled. Trust in God, and trust also in me. ₂There is more than enough room in my Father's home. If it were not so, would I have told you that I am going to prepare a place for you? ₃When everything is ready, I will come and get you, so that you will always be with me where I am. ₄And you know the way to where I am going."

John 14: 1—4 (NLT)

You can't break God's promises by leaning on them.

₂₈ "Come to me, all you who are weary and burdened, and I will give you rest. ₂₉Take my yoke upon you and learn from me, for I am gentle and humble in heart, and you will find rest for your souls. ₃₀For my yoke is easy and my burden is light."

Matthew 11: 28—30 (NIV)

When you are down to nothing, God is up to something.

₁₇By faith Abraham, when put to the test, offered up Isaac. He who had received the promises was ready to offer up his only son, ₁₈ of whom he had been told, "It is through Isaac that descendants shall be named for you." ₁₉He considered the fact that God is able even to raise someone from the dead—and figuratively speaking, he did receives him back.

Hebrews 11: 17—19 (NRSV)

Trust placed in earthly possessions is misplaced trust.

₁₉ "Do not store up for yourselves treasurers on earth, where moth and rust consume and where thieves break in and steal;

Matthew 6: 19 (NRSV)

20The young man said to him, "I have kept all these; what do I still lack?" 21Jesus said to him, "If you wish to be perfect, go, sell your possessions, and give the money to the poor, and you will have treasure in heaven; then come, follow me." 22When the young man heard this word, he went away grieving, for he had many possessions.

Matthew 19: 20—22 (NRSV)

God's Musical Creatures

All we need to do is open our eyes and ears and we can see and hear all of God's creatures.

God's Musical Creatures

The wise old owl sure is cute,
and he'll give us a musical hoot.
Then there is the lonely shrill,
of the far away whippoorwill.
The firefly is pretty quiet, but very bright.
But the cricket's song goes way into the night.

Connie L. Parmenter

Eternal, Eternity

Eternal is forever and never changes, God is eternal.

Thought For The Day

Eternity is without end. Where will you spend eternity?

Eternity/ Eternal Life

God operates on eternal standard time.

8But do not forget this one thing, dear friends: With the Lord a day is like a thousand years, and a thousand years are like a day. 9The Lord is not slow in keeping his promise, as some understand slowness. He is patient with you, not wanting anyone to perish, but everyone to come to repentance.

2nd Peter 3: 8—9 (NIV)

12For there is no distinction between Jew and Greek; the same Lord is Lord of all and is generous to all who call on him. 13For, "Everyone who calls on the name of the Lord shall be saved."

Romans 10: 12—13 (NRSV)

Do you have any idea where you are going? God.

46And these will go away into everlasting punishment, but the righteous into eternal life."

Matthew 25: 46 (NKJV)

8The one who sows to please his sinful nature, from that nature will reap destruction; the one who sows to please the Spirit, from the Spirit will reap eternal life.

Galatians 6:8 (NIV)

Don't waste your life give it to Jesus.

16For God so loved the world that He gave His only begotten Son, that whoever believes in Him should not perish but have everlasting life.

John 3: 16 (NKJV)

23For the wages of sin is death, but the gift of God is eternal life in Christ Jesus our Lord.

Romans 6: 23 (NKJV)

Life is short, eternity isn't.

13Your kingdom is an everlasting kingdom, and your dominion endures throughout all generations.

Psalm 145: 13 (NKJV)

14Why, you do not even know what will happen tomorrow. What is your life? You are a mist that appears for a little while and then vanishes.

James 4: 14 (NIV)

God's gifts are never earned they are deposited.

17Every good and perfect gift is from above, coming down from the Father of the heavenly lights, who does not change like shifting shadows.

James 1:17 (NIV)

No one offers more than God.

8But God proves his love for us in that while we still were sinners Christ died for us.

Romans 5: 8 (NRSV)

13No temptation has overtaken you except such as is common to man; but God is faithful, who will not allow you to be tempted beyond what you are able, but with the temptation will also make the way of escape, that you may be able to bear it.

1st Corinthians 10: 13 (NKJV)

Today's choices have consequences for today and eternity.

28 "Do not be amazed at this, for a time is coming when all who are in their graves will hear his voice 29 and come out—those who have done good will rise to live, and those who have done evil will rise to be condemned.

John 5: 28—29 (NIV)

7Do not be deceived: God cannot be mocked. A man reaps what he sows. 8The one who sows to please his sinful nature, from that nature will reap destruction; the one who sows to please the Spirit, from the Spirit will reap eternal life. 9Let us not become weary in doing good, for at the proper time we will reap a harvest if we do not give up.

Galatians 6: 7—9 (NIV)

Jesus is the only life insurance policy.

6Jesus said to him, "I am the way, the truth, and the life. No one comes to the Father except through me.

John 14: 6 (NKJV)

The church is under the same management for over 2000 years.

8Jesus Christ is the same yesterday, today, and forever.

Hebrews 13: 8 (NKJV)

When facing the Son, you see no shadows.

105Your word is a lamp to my feet and a light for my path.

Psalm 119: 105 (NIV)

5There will be no more night. They will not need the light of a lamp or the light of the sun, for the Lord God will give them light. And they will reign forever and ever.

Revelation 22: 5 (NIV)

When the trumpet sounds, "I'm outta here!"

31And he will send out his angels with the mighty blast of a trumpet, and they will gather his chosen ones from all over the world—from the farthest ends of the earth and heaven.

Matthew 24: 31 (NLT)

52It will happen in a moment, in the blink of an eye, when the last trumpet is blown. For when the trumpet sounds, those who have died will be raised to live forever. And we who are living will be transformed.

1st Corinthians 15: 52 (NLT)

Exposure to the Son can prevent burning.

14 "As Moses lifted up the serpent in the wilderness, even so must the Son of Man be lifted up; 15 so that whoever believes will in Him have eternal life.

John 3: 14—15 (NASB)

It's Then

If you don't have Jesus, God's one and only Son your burdens will always seem heavy, and you will not experience His grace.

Only when you give your heart to Jesus, its then that one day you'll see Him face to face.

It's Then

Sometimes when the load seems heavy
sometimes when the path seems rough.
And I bow beneath a burden,
that seems as if it will crush.

It's then I think of Jesus
who died on Calvary's tree.
And the price that He paid to redeem
a poor lost sinner like me.

It's then that the load seems lighter
and the path seems smooth all the way.
And I hear the voice of the Master's Son,
My grace is sufficient today.

I then turn my eyes toward heaven
and thank God for the gift of His Son.
Whose grace is all sufficient to keep,
till the victories won.

Then someday life's battles will
all be over, and all victories won.
And we can spend eternity with our
heavenly Father in the light of His dear Son.

From my Stepfather
Homer Haley
Written—1980

The Result

Once you accept His Gift—and confess that you are a sinner—to God, you are then accepted by God into His family. You become His child!

12But to all who believe him and accepted him, he gave the right to become children of God.

John 1: 12 (NLT)

18 **"There is no judgment against anyone who believes in him. But anyone who does not believe in him has already been judged for not believing in God's one and only Son.**

John 3: 18 (NLT)

Salvation

We are only saved by God's grace and His mercy.

Thought For The Day

Do you have a right relationship with God? Think about it.

Salvation

Salvation is from God not man.

16 "For God so loved the world that he gave his one and only Son, that whoever believes in him shall not perish but have eternal life.

John 3: 16 (NIV)

8For it is by grace you have been saved, through faith—and this not from yourselves, it is the gift of God—9 not by works, so that no one can boast.

Ephesians 2: 8—9 (NIV)

9 who has saved us and called us to a holy life—not because of anything we have done but because of his own purpose and grace. This grace was given us in Christ Jesus before the beginning of time,

2nd Timothy 1: 9 (NIV)

I can change this sign, only God can change your life.

21 'AND IT SHALL BE THAT EVERYONE WHO CALLS ON THE NAME OF THE LORD WILL BE SAVED.'

Acts 2: 21 (NASB)

1Therefore, having been justified by faith, we have peace with God through our Lord Jesus Christ,

Romans 5: 1 (NASB)

Lost? Come to the cross, get right, go straight.

1Now all the tax collectors and sinners were coming near to listen to him. 2And the Pharisees and the scribes were grumbling and saying, "This fellow welcomes sinners and eats with them." 3So he told them this parable: 4 "Which one of you, having a hundred sheep and losing one of them, does not leave the ninety—nine in the wilderness and go after the one that is lost until he finds it? 5When he has found it, he lays it on his shoulders and rejoices. 6And when he comes home, he calls together his friends and neighbors, saying to them, 'Rejoice with me, for I have found my sheep that was lost.' 7Just so, I tell you, there will be more joy in heaven over one sinner who repents than over ninety-nine righteous persons who need no repentance.

Luke 15: 1—7 (NRSV)

Fire fighters rescue, Jesus saves.

11For the Son of Man has come to save that which was lost.

Matthew 18: 11 (NKJV)

Wal-Mart isn't the only savings place.

12Salvation is found in no one else, for there is no other name under heaven given to men by which we must be saved."

Acts 4: 12 (NIV)

9Much more then, having now been justified by His blood, we shall be saved from the wrath of God through Him.

Romans 5: 9 (NASB)

7In Him we have redemption through His blood, the forgiveness of our trespasses, according to the riches of His grace

Ephesians 1:7 (NASB)

15Here is a trustworthy saying that deserves full acceptance: Christ

Jesus came into the world to save sinners—of whom I am the worst.

1st Timothy 1: 15 (NIV)

When God measurers a man He puts tape around his heart not his head.

10for with the heart a person believes, resulting in righteousness, and with the mouth he confesses, resulting in salvation. 11For the Scriptures says, "WHOEVER BELIEVES IN HIM WILL NOT BE DISAPPOINTED."

Romans 10: 10—11 (NASB)

12For the word of God is living and active and sharper than any two-edged sword, and piercing as far as the division of soul and spirit, of both joints and marrow, and able to judge the thoughts and intentions of the heart.

Hebrews 4: 12 (NASB)

Only a living Savior can rescue can rescue a dying world.

28just as the Son of Man did not come to be served, but to serve, and to give His life a ransom for many."

Matthew 20: 28 (NKJV)

On birthday isn't enough, be born again.

3Jesus answered and said to him, "Most assuredly, I say to you, unless one is born again, he cannot see the kingdom of God." 5Jesus answered, "Most assuredly, I say to you, unless one is born of water and the Spirit, he cannot enter the kingdom of God. 6That which is born of the flesh is flesh, and that which is born of the Spirit is spirit.

John 3: 3, 5—6 (NKJV)

23having been born again, not of corruptible seed but incorruptible, through the word of God which lives and abides forever,

1ˢᵗ Peter1: 23 (NKJV)

Trust Jesus.

12But as many as received Him, to them He gave the right to become children of God, to those who believe in His name:

John 1: 12 (NKJV)

9that if you confess with your mouth the Lord Jesus and believe in your heart that God has raised Him from the dead, you will be saved. 10For with the heart one believes unto righteousness, and with the mouth confession is made unto salvation.

Romans 10: 9—10 (NKJV)

A man is rich according to what he is, not what he has.

4But God is so rich in mercy, and he loved us so much, 5that even though we were dead because of our sins, he gave us life when he raised Christ from the dead. (It is only by God's grace that you have been saved!) 6For he raised us from the dead along with Christ and seated us with him in the heavenly realms because we are united with Christ Jesus. 7So God can point to us in all future ages as examples of the incredible wealth of his grace and kindness toward us, as shown in all he has done for us who are united with Christ Jesus.

Ephesians 2: 4—7 (NLT)

Jesus overcame death, you can too.

21To him who overcomes I will grant to sit with Me on My throne, as I also overcame and sat down with My Father on His throne.

Revelation 3: 21 (NKJV)

God is always a wireless provider.

13For "whoever calls on the name of the LORD shall be saved."

Romans 10: 13 (NKJV)

God's Creation

There is awe in seeing how the snow falls from the sky it seems to float ever so gently to the ground. And awe as we watch the animals playing.

God's Creation

On a cold winter's night the snow is gently falling down,
as the smoke rises from the neighbor's chimneys,
there is no traffic to be found.
Just a rabbit, a doe, and a fawn
making tracks across the snow covered lawn.
Oh! What a feeling of sensation
as we see the beauty of God's creation.

Connie L. Parmenter

Rejoice

Rejoice and smile it's contagious to others around you, so rejoice and be glad in everything.

Thought For The Day

We should rejoice and be thankful for all that we have. Praise God!

Rejoice

A smile adds face value.

₄Rejoice in the Lord always; again I will say, rejoice!

Philippians 4: 4 (NASB)

Take time to laugh its music to your souls

₂₂ₐ A cheerful heart is good medicine,

Proverbs 17: 22a (NIV)

Joy comes in the person of the Lord.

₁₀Then he said to them, "Go, eat of the fat, drink of the sweet, and send portions to him who has nothing prepared; for this day is holy to our Lord. Do not be grieved, for the joy of the LORD is your strength."

Nehemiah 8: 10 (NASB)

₁₁But let all those rejoice who put their trust in You; Let them ever shout for joy, because you defend them; Let those also who love Your name Be joyful in You.

Psalm 5: 11 (NKJV)

An anxious heart weighs a man down, but a cheerful heart lifts him up.

₁₅All the days of the afflicted are bad, But a cheerful heart has a continual feast,

Proverbs 15: 15 (NASB)

It's just as good as, sunshine it's what we call a smile.

₁₃ₐ A happy heart makes the face cheerful,

Proverbs 15:13a (NIV)

Love is what makes you smile when you are tired.

11But let all who take refuge in you rejoice; let them sing joyful praises forever. Spread your protection over them, that all who love your name may be filled with joy.

Psalm 5: 11 (NLT)

Enjoy today, complements of God.

24This is the day which the LORD has made; Let us rejoice and be glad in it.

Psalm 118: 24 (NASB)

There's always something to be thankful for.

16Rejoice always, 17pray without ceasing, 18give thanks in all circumstances; for this is the will of God in Christ Jesus for you.

1st Thessalonians 5: 16—18 (NRSV)

Thanksgiving

Thanksgiving is a day when families usually get together and have a big dinner with turkey and all the trimmings. However there are many who don't have a family to gather with or maybe they are in prison or a hospital or a nursing home.

They may not have that turkey and all the trimmings. However they can also be thankful for what they do have. We can share our food with them and also share Jesus with them as well.

If we have Jesus in our hearts we should be the most thankful of all, because if you have Jesus you have everything.

Thanksgiving

Some folks think of Thanksgiving as just only that one day
is clear, but Thanksgiving should be each day of the year.

God has given us many blessings, and each day they do mount.

So each day throughout the year, your
many blessings you should count.

Have you counted your many blessings each day through?

And have you thought about what God has done for you?

Then you need to be on your knees and give God
the praise, for these are all Thanksgiving days.

Connie L. Parmenter

Prayer

Prayer is talking with the Lord, anywhere, anytime, about anything.

Thought For The Day

Do you have a prayer life?

You should have. Try it!

Prayer

God, "can we talk?"

3 'Call to Me and I will answer you, and I will tell you great and mighty things, which you do not know.' Jeremiah 33:3 (NASB)

14This is the confidence which we have before Him, that, if we ask anything according to His will, He hears us. 15And if we know that He hears us in whatever we ask, we know that we have the requests which we have asked from Him.

1ˢᵗ John 5: 14—15 (NASB

ASAP = Always say a prayer.

6Be anxious for nothing, but in everything by prayer and supplication with thanksgiving let your requests be made known to God. 7And the peace of God, which surpasses all comprehension, will guard your hearts and your minds in Christ Jesus.

Philippians 4: 6—7 (NASB)

If you can't sleep, don't count sheep, talk to the Shepherd.

6On my bed I remember you; I think of you through the watches of the night.

Psalm 63: 6 (NIV)

When life knocks you to your knees pray there.

17The righteous cry, and the LORD hears And delivers them out of all their troubles. 18The LORD is near to the brokenhearted And saves those who are crushed in spirit.

Psalm 34: 17—18 (NASB)

13Are any among you suffering? They should pray. Are any cheerful? They should sing songs of praise.

James 5: 13 (NRSV)

Prayer is a spiritual exercise. Are you in shape?

40Then he returned to the disciples and found them asleep. He said to Peter, "Couldn't you watch with me even one hour? 41Keep watch and pray, so that you will not give in to temptation. For the spirit is willing, but the body is weak!"

Matthew 26: 40—41 (NLT)

26And the Holy Spirit helps us in our weakness. For example, we don't know what God wants us to pray for. But the Holy Spirit prays for us with groaning that cannot be expressed in words.

Romans 8: 26 (NLT)

38Keep watch and pray, so that you will not give in to temptation. For the spirit is willing, but the body is weak."

Mark 14: 38 (NLT)

Back sliding starts when knee bending stops.

3So I gave my attention to the Lord God to seek Him by prayer and supplications, with fasting, sackcloth and ashes. 4I prayed to the LORD my God and confessed and said, "Alas, O Lord, the great and awesome God, who keeps His covenant and loving-kindness for those who love Him and keep His commandments,

Daniel 9: 3—4 (NASB)

Help is just a prayer away.

3Morning by morning, O LORD, you hear my voice; morning by morning I lay my requests before you and wait in expectation.

James 5: 3 (NIV)

13And I will do whatever you ask in my name, so that the Son may bring glory to the Father. 14You may ask me for anything in my name, and I will do it.

John 14: 13—14 (NIV)

Unload baggage here. Pray.

6Do not be anxious about anything, but in everything, by prayer and petition, with thanksgiving, present your requests to God.

Philippians 4: 6 (NIV)

Much kneeling will keep you in good standing.

18Pray in the Spirit at all times and on every occasion. Stay alert and be persistent in your prayers for all believers everywhere.

Ephesians 6: 18 (NLT)

Pray about everything, worry about nothing.

7Give all your worries and cares to God, for he cares about you.

1st Peter 5:7 (NLT)

It's hard to stumble when you are on your knees.

14and My people who are called by My name humble themselves and pray and seek My face and turn from their wicked ways, then I will hear from heaven, will forgive their sin and will heal their land.

2nd Chronicles 7: 14 (NASB)

41 "Keep watching and praying that you may not enter into temptation; the spirit is willing, but the flesh is weak."

Matthew 26:41 (NASB)

The best way to remember someone is in prayer.

25Dear brothers and sisters, pray for us.

1st Thessalonians 5: 25 (NLT)

16Confess your sins to each other and pray for each other so that you may be healed. The earnest prayer of a righteous person has great power and produces wonderful results.

James 5: 16 (NLT)

P—pray U—until S—something H—happens .

17Elijah was a human being like us, and he prayed fervently that it might not rain, and for three years and six months it did not rain on the earth. 18Then he prayed again, and the heaven gave rain and the earth yielded its harvest.

James 5: 17—18 (NRSV)

Prayer: Reporting for duty.

18With all prayer and petition pray at all times in the Spirit, and with this in view, be on the alert with all perseverance and petition for all the saints,

Ephesians 6: 18 (NASB)

17Pray without ceasing;

1st Thessalonians 5: 17 (NASB)

Impossible? Call on the power of God.

26Jesus looked at them intently and said, "Humanly speaking, it is impossible. But with God everything is possible."

Matthew 19: 26 (NLT)

God's answers are wiser than our prayers

8 "So do not be like them; for the Father knows what you need before you ask Him.

Matthew 6: 8 (NASB)

5If you need wisdom, ask our generous God, and he will give it to you. He will not rebuke you for asking. 6But when you ask him, be sure that your faith is in God alone. Do not waver, for a person with divided loyalty is as unsettled as a wave of the sea that is blown and tossed by the wind. 7Such people should not expect to receive anything from the Lord. 8Their loyalty is divided between God and the world, and they are unstable in everything they do.

James 1: 5—8 (NLT)

Show Me The Way

Lord teach us how to tell others about you and your Kingdom. How we each can know you better, and teach us how to pray for others in your name.

As we read Your Word speak to our hearts and direct us for your glory. And we thank you for your grace to us.

Show Me The Way

Show me the way not to fortune or fame,
not how to win laurels or praise for my name.
But show me the way to spread, "The Great Story"
that is thine, The Kingdom, the power and glory.

If we send no ships out, no ships will come in,
and unless there's a contest nobody can win.
For games can't be won unless they are played,
and prayers can't be answered unless they are prayed.

No one ever sought the Father and found He wasn't there,
and no burden is too heavy to be lightened by prayer.
No problem is too intricate, and no sorrow that we face,
is too deep and devastating, to be softened by His grace.

From my Stepfather
Homer Haley
Written—1980

Now what

That's it! There is nothing else required to get to heaven, and live eternally with God and escape hell. BUT, that does not mean that you only have fire insurance. This decision should make you not want to go on living your life the way you want to.

There are a few things God asks you to do. These are not demands, and if you choose not to do them, your decision to accept Jesus payment will still remain intact.

He loves you and wants to build a relationship with you.

27God did this so that men would seek him and perhaps reach out for him and find him, though he is not far from any one of us.

Acts 17:27 (NIV)

Pray to Him daily.

16Be joyful always; 17pray continually; 18give thanks in all circumstances, for this is God's will for you in Christ Jesus.

1st Thessalonians 5: 16—18 (NIV)

Read the Bible.

₄Jesus answered, "It is written: 'Man does not live on bread alone, but on every word that comes from the mouth of God.' "

Matthew 4: 4 (NIV)

He wants you to show others that you have made the decision to accept Jesus death as payment for your penalty, so He asks you to be baptized.

₁₅**You will be his witness to all men of what you have seen and heard.** ₁₆**And now what are you waiting for? Get up, be baptized and wash your sins away, calling on his name.'**

Acts 22: 15—16 (NIV)

He wants you to tell others that Jesus' payment is for their sins also.

₁₄**But how can they call on him to save them unless they believe in him? And how can they believe in him if they have never heard about him? And how can they hear about him unless someone tells them?**

Romans 10: 14 (NLT)

He knows that your life will not be easy, so He asks you to attend church and meet with other Christians and get support from them.

₂₄**And let us consider how we may spur one another on toward love and good deeds.** ₂₅**Let us not give up meeting together, as some are in the habit of doing, but let us encourage one another—and all the more as you see the Day approaching.**

Hebrews 10: 24—25 (NIV)

This is not a checklist of To Do's, but rather a few things you will want to do as you get to know Jesus better. As you go to church, you will learn many things that will help you grow closer in your relationship and lead a better life. Find a church that teaches the Bible, not just a place that refers to it. Find a place that is welcoming, and where the others want to help you learn and grow closer to Jesus.

Word Of God

The Word of God is the Bible and should be read each day.

Thought For The Day

Do you read your Bible? If not, how can you get to know God?

Word Of God

Truth will stand long after opinions cease.

160All your words are true; all your righteous laws are eternal.

Psalm 119: 160 (NIV)

31Then Jesus said to those Jews who believed Him, "If you abide in My word, you are My disciples indeed. 32And you shall know the truth, and the truth shall make you free." 36Therefore if the Son makes you free, you shall be free indeed.

John 8: 31—32, 36 (NKJV)

If you are searching for nuggets of truth, the Bible is a gold mine.

Read it!

The Bible's treasures can only be found by those who dig from them.

19It is to be with him, and he is to read it all the days of his life so that he may learn to revere the LORD his God and follow carefully all the words of this law and these decrees

Deuteronomy 17:19 (NIV)

97Oh, how I love your law! I meditate on it all day long.

Psalm 119: 97 (NIV)

The Bible fits man for life and prepares him for death.

23Rejoice in that day and leap for joy, for surely your reward is great in heaven; for that is what their ancestors did to the prophets.

Luke 6: 23 (NRSV)

15You have been taught the Holy Scriptures from childhood, and they have given you the wisdom to receive the salvation that comes by trusting in Christ Jesus. 16All Scripture is inspired by God and is useful to teach us what is true and make us realize what is wrong in our lives. It corrects us when we are wrong and teaches us to do what is right.

2nd Timothy 3: 15—16 (NLT)

Spend less time on face book, and more time in His Book.

12Indeed, the word of God is living and active, sharper than any two-edged sword, piercing until it divides soul from spirit, joints from marrow; it is able to judge the thoughts and intentions of the heart.

Hebrews 4: 12 (NRSV)

Rules of the road of life are found in the Bible.

6 'I am the LORD your God who brought you out of the land of Egypt, out of the house of bondage. 7 'You shall have no other gods before Me. 8 'You shall not make for yourself a carved image—any likeness of anything that is in heaven above, or that is in the earth beneath, or that is in the water under the earth; 9 you shall not bow down to them nor serve them. For I, the LORD your God, am a jealous God, visiting the iniquity of the fathers upon the children to the third and fourth generations of those who hate Me, 10 but showing mercy to thousands, to those who love Me and keep My commandments. 11 'You shall not take the name of the LORD your God in vain, for the LORD will not hold him guiltless who takes His name in vain.12 'Observe the Sabbath day, to keep it holy, as the LORD your God commanded you. 13Six days you shall labor and do all your work, 14 but the seventh day is the Sabbath of the LORD your God. In it you shall do no work: you, nor your son, nor your daughter, nor your male

servant, nor your female servant, nor your ox, nor your donkey, nor any of your cattle, nor your stranger who is within your gates, that your male servant and your female servant may rest as well as you. 15And remember that you were a slave in the land of Egypt, and the LORD your God brought you out from there by a mighty hand and by an outstretched arm; therefore the LORD your God commanded you to keep the Sabbath day. 16 'Honor your father and your mother, as the LORD your God has commanded you, that your days may be long, and that it may be well with you in the land which the LORD your God is giving you. 17 'You shall not murder. 18 'You shall not commit adultery. 19'You shall not steal. 20'You shall not bear false witness against your neighbor. 21 'You shall not covet your neighbor's wife; and you shall not desire your neighbor's house, his field, his male servant, his female servant, his ox, his donkey, or anything that is your neighbor's.'

Deuteronomy 5; 6—21 (NKJV)

God only wrote one Book. Don't you think you should read it?

What do you think?

Feed your faith and your doubts will starve to death.

15Do your best to present yourself to God as one approved, a workman who does not need to be ashamed and who correctly handles the word of truth.

2nd Timothy 2: 15 (NIV)

6And without faith it is impossible to please God, because anyone who comes to him must believe that he exists and that he rewards those who earnestly seek him.

Hebrews 11: 6 (NIV)

The Ten Commandments are a map not a trap.

1Therefore, there is now no condemnation for those who are in Christ Jesus, 2 because through Christ Jesus the law of the Spirit of life set me free from the law of sin and death. 3For what the law was powerless to do in that it was weakened by the sinful nature, God did by sending his own Son in the likeness of sinful man to be a sin offering. And so he condemned sin in sinful man, 4 in order that the righteous requirements of the law might be fully met in us, who do not live according to the sinful nature but according to the Spirit.

Romans 8: 1—4 (NIV)

Nothing is politically right that is morally wrong.

43 "You have heard that it was said, 'You shall love your neighbor and hate your enemy.' 44But I say to you, Love your enemies and pray for those who persecute you, 45 so that you may be children of your Father in heaven; for he makes his sun rise on the evil and on the good, and sends rain on the righteous and on the unrighteous. 46For if you love those who love you, what reward do you have? Do not even the tax collectors do the same? 47And if you greet only your brothers and sisters, what more are you doing than others? Do not even the Gentiles do the same? 48Be perfect, therefore, as your heavenly Father is perfect.

Matthew 5:43—48 (NRSV)

Prevent truth decay, brush up on the Bible.

4But he answered, "It is written, 'One does not live by bread alone, but by every word that comes from the mouth of God.'"

Matthew 4: 4 (NRSV)

14But as for you, continue in what you have learned and firmly believed , knowing from whom you learned it, 15 and how from childhood you have known the sacred writings that are able to instruct you for salvation through faith in Christ Jesus. 16All scripture is inspired by God and is useful for teaching, for reproof, for correction, and for training in righteousness,

2nd Timothy 3: 14—15 (NRSV)

Look to the word to fill your needs instead of the world.

1In your strength the king rejoices, O LORD, and in your help how greatly he exults!

Psalm 21: 1 (NRSV)

8Do not be like them, for your Father knows what you need before you ask him. 32For it is the Gentiles who strive for all these things; and indeed your heavenly Father knows that you need all these things. 33But strive first for the kingdom of God and his righteousness, and all these things will be given to you as well.

Matthew 6: 8, 32—33 (NRSV)

19And my God will fully satisfy every need of yours according to his riches in glory in Christ Jesus.

Philippians 4: 19 (NRSV)

Need to read a Good Book? Come on in, we use the world's Best Seller.

160The very essence of your words is truth; all your just regulations will stand forever.

Psalm 119: 160 (NLT)

39 "You search the Scriptures because you think they give you eternal life. But the Scriptures point to me!

John 5: 39 (NLT)

The Bible is the story of God, and His people.

Find out what It says!

The more you read the Bible the more you'll love the author.

16All scripture is inspired by God and is useful for teaching, for reproof, for correction, and for training in righteousness,

2ⁿᵈ Timothy 3: 16 (NRSV)

20First of all you must understand this, that no prophecy of scripture is a matter of one's own interpretation, 21 because no prophecy ever came by human will, but men and women moved by the Holy Spirit spoke from God.

2ⁿᵈ Peter 1: 20—21 (NRSV)

The Preacher And The Lady

We all need to read the little black Book the Bible as Christians we should also tell others about God. We may not be "preachers" but we can all be God's messengers.

The Preacher and the Lady

The preacher is a man of God, as he travels on this sod.

He took his little black Book and he did read,
so he would know the Master's creed.

One day he thought he'd take a wife (maybe).
Then he met this beautiful lady.

They did court for awhile, and in his usual style,
he asked her for her hand. She said," yes you're the man."

This marriage God did bless and they had
four lovely girls as you can guess.

Much time has passed since then and
he preaches again and again.

Now it's time for them to go, a different
pulpit the Lord does bestow.

We will miss their smiling faces, but we pray
for them the Lords wonderful graces.

Oh! Yes, that little black Book, they both read daily.

The preacher and the lady.

Connie L. Parmenter

Witnessing

Witnessing is telling others about the Lord and what He has done for them and you.

Thought For The Day

Are you telling others what God has done for you? You should, it's what He wants you to do.

Witnessing

A candle looses nothing by lighting another candle.

41Those who believed what Peter said were baptized and added to the church that day—about 3,000 in all.

Acts 2: 41 (NLT)

7So God's message continued to spread. The number of believers greatly increased in Jerusalem, and many of the Jewish priests were converted, too.

Acts 6: 7 (NLT)

God doesn't take a vacation from you.

18Jesus came and told his disciples, "I have been given all authority in heaven and on earth. 19Therefore, go and make disciples of all nations, baptizing them in the name of the Father and the Son and the Holy Spirit. 20Teach these new disciples to obey all the commands I have given you. And be sure of this: I am with you always, even to the end of the age."

Matthew 28: 18—10 (NLT)

There's no better sermon than a good example.

16Let your light so shine before men, that they may see your good works and glorify your Father in heaven.

Matthew 5: 16 (NKJV)

7For you yourselves know how you ought to follow our example. We were not idle when we were with you, 8 nor did we eat anyone's food without paying for it. On the contrary, we worked night and day, laboring and toiling so that we would not be a burden to any of you. 9We did this, not because we do not have the right to such help, but in order to make ourselves a model for you to follow.

2nd Thessalonians 3: 7—9 (NIV)

Why go out on a limb? Because that's, where the fruit is.

37He said to his disciples," The harvest is great, but the workers are few. 38So pray to the Lord who is in charge of the harvest; ask him to send more workers into the fields."

Matthew 9: 37—38 (NLT)

8But you will receive power when the Holy Spirit comes upon you. And you will be my witness, telling people about me everywhere— in Jerusalem, throughout Judea, in Samaria, and to the ends of the earth."

Acts 1:8 (NLT)

We were born to be witnesses, not lawyers or judges.

18 And Jesus came and spoke to them, saying, "All authority has been given to Me in heaven and on earth. 19Go therefore and make disciples of all the nations, baptizing them in the name of the Father and of the Son and of the Holy Spirit, 20 teaching them to observe all things that I have commanded you; and lo, I am with you always, even to the end of the age." Amen.

Matthew 28: 18—20 (NKJV)

1 "Judge not, that you be not judged. 2For with what judgment you judge, you will be judged; and with the measure you use, it will be measured back to you.

Matthew 7: 1—2 (NKJV)

Christians worth their salt causes others to be thirsty.

6Let your speech always be gracious, seasoned with salt, so that you may know how you ought to answer everyone.

Colossians 4:6 (NRSV)

We plant, we water, God makes it grows.

6I planted the seed in your hearts, and Apollos watered it, but it was God who made it grow. 7It's not important who does the planting, or who does the watering. What's important is that God makes the seed grow.

1st Corinthians 3: 6—7 (NLT)

He who kneels before God, can stand before anyone.

14We all fell down, and I heard a voice saying to me in Aramaic, 'Saul, Saul, why are you persecuting me? It is useless for you to fight against my will.' 15 " ' Who are you, lord?' I asked. "And the Lord replied, 'I am Jesus, the one you are persecuting. 16Now get to your feet! For I have appeared to you to appoint you as my servant and witness. You are to tell the world what you have seen and what I will show you in the future. 17And I will rescue you from both your own people and the Gentiles. Yes, I am sending you to the Gentiles. 18to open their eyes, so they may turn from darkness to light and from the power of Satan to God. Then they will receive forgiveness for their sins and be given a place among God's people, who are set apart by faith in me.' 19 "And so, King Agrippa, I obeyed that vision from heaven. 20I preached first to those in Damascus, then in Jerusalem and throughout all Judea, and also to the Gentiles, that all must repent of their sins and turn to God—and prove they have changed by the good things they do.

Acts 26: 14—20 (NLT)

Choices

We all have many choices in this life but there are only two choices that deal with eternity.

Thought For The Day

If you choose Jesus and give your life to Him then heaven is the result. But if you do not choose Jesus then you have Satan and the result is hell—forever. The choice is yours and only yours make your choice now, you may not have tomorrow.

Choices

Try Jesus if you don't like Him, the devil will always take you back.

14Then one of the twelve, named Judas Iscariot, went to the chief priest 15 and said, "What are you willing to give me to betray Him to you?" And they weighed out thirty pieces of silver to him.16From then on he began looking for a good opportunity to betray Jesus.

Matthew 26: 14—16 (NASB)

20 "Truly, truly, I say to you, he who receives whomever I send receives Me; and he who receives Me receives Him who sent Me." 21When Jesus had said this, He was troubled in spirit, and testified and said, "Truly, truly, I say to you, that one of you will betray Me,"

John 13: 20—21 (NASB)

He is no genius who ignores his Creator.

14They say to God, 'Leave us alone! We do not desire to know your ways.

Job 21: 14 (NLT)

1Fools say in their hearts, "There is no God." They are corrupt, they commit abominable acts; there is no one who does good.

Psalm 53: 1 (NLT)

5But they deliberately forget that long ago by God's word the heavens existed and the earth was formed out of water and with water.

2nd Peter 3: 5 (NIV)

Life has many choices, eternity has two. What's yours?

15And if it seems evil to you to serve the LORD, choose for

yourselves this day whom you will serve, whether the gods which your fathers served that were on the other side of the River, or the gods of the Amorites, in whose land you dwell. But as for me and my house, we will serve the LORD.

Joshua 24: 15 (NKJV)

30I have chosen the way of truth; Your judgments I have laid before me.

Psalm 119; 30 (NKJV)

Enjoy today it won't be back.

24This is the day which the LORD has made; Let us rejoice and be glad in it.

Psalm 118: 24 (NASB)

13But encourage one another day after day, as long as it is still called "Today," so that none of you will be hardened by the deceitfulness of sin.

Hebrews 3: 13 (NASB)

Attitude is everything, pick a good one.

24Then Jesus said to His disciples, "If anyone wishes to come after Me, he must deny himself, and take up his cross and follow Me. 25 "For whoever wishes to save his life will lose it; but whoever loses his life for My sake will find it.

Matthew 16: 24—25 (NASB)

23Jesus answered and said to him, "If anyone loves Me, he will keep My word; and My Father will love him, and We will come to him and make Our home with him.

John 14:23 (NKJV)

21For you have been called for this purpose, since Christ also suffered for you, leaving you an example for you to follow in His steps,

1st Peter 2: 21 (NASB)

Include God in your plans, you are in His.

14Yet you do not even know what tomorrow will bring. What is your life? For you are a mist that appears for a little while and then vanishes. 15Instead you ought to say, "If the Lord wishes, we will live and do this or that."

James 4: 14—15 (NRSV)

If you feel far from God! Who moved?

4Come near to God and he will come near to you. Wash your hands, you sinners, and purify your hearts, you double-minded.

James 4: 8 (NIV)

Silence is golden, it cannot be repeated.

13Then keep your tongue from speaking evil and your lips from telling lies!

Psalm 34: 13 (NLT)

23Watch your tongue and keep your mouth shut, and you will stay out of trouble.

Proverbs 21: 23 (NLT)

10For, "Whoever would love life and see good days must keep his tongue from evil and his lips from deceitful speech.

1st Peter 3: 10 (NIV)

You can't hold hands with God and hold hands with the devil.

24 "No one can serve two masters; for either he will hate the one and love the other, or he will be devoted to the one and despise the other. You cannot serve both God and wealth.

Matthew 6: 24 (NASB)

Don't ever give Satan a ride he'll always want to drive.

7So humble yourselves before God. Resist the devil, and he will flee from you.

James 4:7 (NLT)

27and do not give the devil an opportunity.

Ephesians 4: 27 (NASB)

11Put on the full armor of God, so that you will able to stand firm against the schemes of the devil.

Ephesians 6: 11 (NASB)

A grudge is too heavy a load to carry.

9do not grumble against one another, brethren, lest you be condemned. Behold the Judge is standing at the door!

James 5: 9 (NKJV)

Famous last words: "later."

1Do not boast about tomorrow, For you do not know what a day may bring forth.

Proverbs 27:1 (NASB)

14How do you know what your life will be like tomorrow? Your life is like the morning fog—it's here a little while, then it's gone.

James 4: 14 (NLT)

I died for you will you live for me? Jesus.

4We were therefore buried with him through baptism into death in order that, just as Christ was raised from the dead through the glory of the Father, we too may live a new life.

Romans 6:4 (NIV)

13Therefor, prepare your minds for action; be self-controlled; set your hope fully on the grace to be given you when Jesus is revealed.

1st Peter 1: 13 (NIV)

Contentment is not getting what you want it's being satisfied with what you have.

6Yet true godliness with contentment is itself great wealth. 7After all, we brought nothing with us when we come into the world, and we can't take anything with us when we leave it. 8So if we have enough food and clothing, let us be content. 9But people who long to be rich fall into temptation and are trapped by many foolish and harmful desires that plunge them into ruin and destruction. 10For the love of money is the root of all kinds of evil. And some people, craving money, have wandered from the true faith and pierced themselves with many sorrows.

1st Timothy 6: 6—10 (NLT)

Those who fly into a rage, always have a bad landing.

19My dear brothers, take note of this: Everyone should be quick to listen, slow to speak and slow to become angry, 20for man's anger does not bring about the righteous life that God desires.

James 1: 19—20 (NIV)

Those who follow the crowd, soon become part of the crowd.

20He who walks with wise men will be wise, But the companion of fools will suffer harm.

Proverbs 13: 20 (NASB)

17As iron sharpens iron, so one man sharpens another.

Proverbs 27: 17 (NIV)

When a man drinks to forget, he usually forgets to stop.

1Wine is a mocker, strong drink a brawler, And whoever is intoxicated by it is not wise.

Proverbs 20: 1 (NASB)

A closed mouth holds no foot.

17A quick—tempered man does foolish things, and a crafty man is hated.

Proverbs 14: 17 (NIV)

11A fool always loses his temper, But a wise man holds it back.

Proverbs 29: 11 (NASB)

Heaven or hell, Joy or misery?

19I call heaven and earth to witness against you today that I have set before you life and death, blessings and curses. Choose life so that you and your descendants may live,

Deuteronomy 30: 19 (NRSV)

Freedom to do as you ought, not as you please.

16For you are free, yet you are God's slaves, so don't use your freedom as an excuse to do evil.

1st Peter 2: 16 (NLT)

17Anyone, then, who knows the right thing to do and fails to do it, commits sin.

James 4: 17 (NRSV)

Money is a helpful servant, but a cruel master.

16A little that a righteous man has Is better than the riches of many wicked.

Psalm 37: 16 (NKJV)

16Better is a little with the fear of the LORD, Than great treasure with trouble.

Proverbs 15: 16 (NKJV)

On the bench or in the game?

30 "He who is not with me is against me, and he who does not gather with me scatters.

Matthew 12: 30 (NIV)

15Do your best to present yourself to God as one approved, a workman who does not need to be ashamed and who correctly handles the word of truth.

2nd Timothy 2: 15 (NIV)

We cannot direct the wind, but we can adjust our sails.

21Elijah said to the people and said, " How long will you waver between two opinions? If the LORD is God, follow him; but if Baal is God, follow him." But the people said nothing.

1st Kings 18: 21 (NIV)

2Don't copy the behavior and customs of this world, but let God transform you into a new person by changing the way you think. Then you will learn to know God's will for you, which is good and pleasing and perfect.

Romans 12: 2 (NLT)

God wants full custody, not just week-end visitation.

2Yet day after day they seek me and delight to know my ways, as if they were a nation that practiced righteousness and did not forsake the ordinance of their God; they ask of me righteous judgments, they delight to draw near to God.

Isaiah 58: 2 (NRSV)

11These Jews were more receptive than those in Thessalonica, for they welcomed the message very eagerly and examined the scriptures every day to see whether these things were so.

Acts 17: 11 (NRSV)

If we pause to think we'll pause to thank.

12I thank Christ Jesus our Lord, who has strengthened me, because He considered me faithful, putting me into service,

1st Timothy 1: 12 (NASB)

₄For everything created by God is g od, and nothing is to be rejected if it is received with gratitude;

1ˢᵗ Timothy 4: 4 (NASB)

The devil's trick is no treat.

₁The serpent was the shrewdest of all the wild animals the LORD God had made. One day he asked the woman, "Did God really say you must not eat the fruit from any of the trees in the garden?"

Genesis 3: 1 (NLT)

If you're too busy to read the Bible, you're too busy.

₁₆All Scripture is inspired by God and is useful to teach us what is true and to make us realize what is wrong in our lives. It corrects us when we are wrong and teaches us to do what is right.

2ⁿᵈ Timothy 3:16 (NLT)

God or Satan? There is no middle ground.

₆The mind of sinful man is death, but the mind controlled by the Spirit is life and peace; ₇ the sinful mind is hostile to God. It does not submit to God's law, nor can it do so. ₈Those controlled by the sinful nature cannot please God.

Romans 8: 6—8 (NIV)

Choices And Changes

We all make choices every day some choices are not as good as others. So with God's help we can also make changes to glorify Him.

Choices and Changes

If God can change the seasons
from winter, spring, summer and fall.
Then when we believe in Jesus
and ask Him into our heart,
He can change us one and all from the very start.

We can see the beauty He has given us in each season,
and with Jesus! Others can see Him in us for this very reason.
So there is no real excuse for you not to ask Him in,
For if you have Jesus, you win and win and win!

Whatever our choice, we each are libel,
for God has given us the very best
Guide Book, the Bible!

So think about the time when Jesus will come,
and where you will spend eternity!
The choice is yours as you know well.
Will it be forever with God in Heaven
or separated from Him forever in Hell?

Connie L. Parmenter

Plan of Salvation

Man's Problem

No matter what you have done in your life, or how much good you have done, or how much you have served or given money to help others, we all have the same problem—we are separated from God.

2It's your sins that have cut you off from God. Because of your sins, he has turned away and will not listen any more.

Isaiah 59: 2 (NLT)

It does not matter to God if you only told a little white lie, or committed murder. It is all sin—and we have all sinned.

23For everyone has sinned; we all fall short of God's glorious standard.

Romans 3: 23 (NLT)

He cannot allow sin in His presence. Worse yet, there is a penalty for sin.

23For the wages of sin is death, but the gift of God is eternal life in Christ Jesus our Lord.

Romans 6: 23 (NIV)

We Cannot Work our Way to God

It is easy to want to find a way to do something to earn our way to God. It doesn't seem fair. If I got myself into this mess, then I should be able to get out of it. But no good works will ever be enough to get to God.

5He saved us, not because of the righteous things we had done, but because of his mercy.

Titus 3:5a (NLT)

5God saved you by his grace when you believed. And you can't take credit for this; it is a gift from God. 9Salvation is not a reward for the good things we have done, so none of us can boast about it.

Ephesians 2: 8—9 (NLT)

God has a solution

Since we cannot do anything to earn our way to God, He loved us so much that He provided a way that we can live with Him.

8But God demonstrates his own love for us in this: While we were still sinners, Christ died for us.

Romans 5: 8 (NIV)

25He was handed over to die because of our sins, and he was raised to life to make us right with God.

Romans 4:25 (NLT)

16 **"For God loved the world so much that he gave his one and only Son, so that everyone who believes in him will not parish but have eternal life.**

John 3: 16 (NLT)

The important part to remember, though, is that there is only one solution. We cannot add anything to it or find a way around it.

6Jesus told him, "I am the way, the truth, and the life. No one can come to the Father except through me.

John 14: 6 (NLT)

Accept His Gift

Since Jesus is the only way to God, you need to do only one thing—accept Jesus' death as the replacement for the penalty of your sins. All you have to do is believe that His death is enough.

31They replied, "Believe in the Lord Jesus and you will be saved, along with everyone in your household."

Acts 16: 31 (NLT)

9If you confess with your mouth that Jesus is Lord and believe in your heart that God raised him from the dead, you will be saved. 10For it is by believing in your heart that you are made right with God, and it is by confessing with your mouth that you are saved.

Romans 10: 9—10 (NLT)

The Result

Once you accept His Gift—and confess that you are a sinner—to God, you are then accepted by God into His family. You become His child!

₁₂**But to all who believed him and accepted him, he gave the right to become children of God.**

John 1: 12 (NLT)

₁₈ **"There is no judgment against anyone who believes in him. But anyone who does not believe in him has already been judged for not believing in God's one and only Son.**

John 3: 18 (NLT)

Now What?

That's it! There is nothing else required to get to heaven, and live eternally with God and escape hell. BUT, that does not mean that you only have fire insurance. This decision should make you not want to go on living your life the way you want to.

There are a few things God asks you to do. These are not demands, and if you choose not to do them, your decision to accept Jesus payment will still remain intact.

He loves you and wants to build a relationship with you.

27**God did this so that men would seek him and perhaps reach out for him and find him, though he is not far from any one of us.**

Acts 17: 27 (NIV)

Pray to Him daily.

16**Be joyful always;** 17 **pray continually;** 18 **give thanks in all circumstances, for this is God's will for you in Christ Jesus.**

1st Thessalonians 5: 16—18 (NIV)

Read the Bible.

₄Jesus answered, "It is written: 'Man does not live on bread alone, but on every word that comes from the mouth of God.' "

Matthew 4: 4 (NIV)

He wants you to show others that you have made the decision to accept Jesus death as payment for your penalty, so He asks you to be baptized.

₁₅You will be his witness to all men of what you have seen and heard.₁₆And now what are you waiting for? Get up, be baptized and wash your sins away, calling on his name.'

Acts 22: 15—16 (NIV)

He wants you to tell others that Jesus' payment is for their sins also.

₁₄But how can they call on him to save them unless they believe in him? And how can they believe in him if they have never heard about him? And how can they hear about him unless someone tells them?

Romans 10: 14 (NLT)

He knows that your life will not be easy, so He asks you to attend church and meet with other Christians and get support from them.

₂₄And let us consider how we may spur one another on toward love and good deeds. ₂₅Let us not give up meeting together, as some are in the habit of doing, but let us encourage one another—and all the more as you see the Day approaching.

Hebrews 10: 24—25 (NIV)

This is not a check list of To Do's, but rather a few things you will want to do as you get to know Jesus better. As you go to church, you will learn many things that will help you grow closer in your relationship and lead a better life. Find a church that teaches from the Bible, not just a place that refers to it. Find a place that is welcoming, and where the others want to help you learn and grow closer to Jesus.

When you're out and about

When you drive past a church be sure to read the sayings on the church signs, because it may just spark something in your heart.

Maybe it will be God speaking to you, if you feel God nudging your heart to go to church, to read His Word or to give your life to Him don't say no.

Even if you don't quite understand everything you read that's ok because no one ever understands it all. Except God!

But if you ask Jesus into your heart, the Holy Spirit will help you to know more each time you read the Bible, when you pray and ask Him to help you He will.

Each day ask God for wisdom to help you through the day for daily decisions you may need to make and to help you tell others about Him.

God Bless you as you read this book.

CPSIA information can be obtained
at www.ICGtesting.com
Printed in the USA
FSOW01n1010020215
4959FS

9 781490 823027